MW00761424

A GUIDE TO OBTAINING A PSYCHOLOGY INTERNSHIP

SECOND EDITION

Revised and Expanded

Edwin I. Megargee, Ph.D.
Director of Clinical Training
Florida State University

ACCELERATED DEVELOPMENT INC.
Publishers
Muncie   Indiana

A GUIDE TO OBTAINING
A PSYCHOLOGY INTERNSHIP

SECOND EDITION
Revised and Expanded

© Copyright 1992 by Accelerated Development Inc.

10   9   8   7   6   5   4   3   2   1

Printed in the United States of America.

All rights reserved. No part of this book may be reproduced
or transmitted in any form or means, electronic or mechanical,
including photocopying, recording, or by an informational
storage and retrieval system, without permission in writing
from Acclerated Development Inc.

Technical Development: Tanya Benn
                         Cynthia Long
                         Marguerite Mader
                         Shaeney Pigman
                         Sheila Sheward

ISBN: 1-55959-043-2

ACCELERATED DEVELOPMENT INC.
PUBLISHERS
3808 West Kilgore Avenue
Muncie, IN 47304-4896
Telephone (317)-284-7511
Toll Free Order Number 1-800-222-1166

PREFACE

Each year approximately 2,000 psychology graduate students apply for predoctoral internships in professional psychology. Recently they prepared and filed over 23,000 individual applications as they competed for 1,859 APA-accredited and 314 non-accredited positions. This vast, confusing selection process lasts for almost six months, and, according to the Dean of a school of professional psychology, this " ...annual selection madness... results in unnecessary anxiety aggravation and expense (Fox, 1991, p. 34). He concludes that something should be done.

This book was written in response to that need. It will not cure the system's madness or get rid of the "bozos" Fox complains about, but it has helped students cope with the system successfully. Completely rewritten and revised to incorporate the latest data on internship selection and the most recent rules governing the selection process, this Second Edition of A Guide To Obtaining A Psychology Internship:

1. Discloses the political   and power relations among internship training directors, university faculties, and internship applicants, and describes how they influence the APPIC Guidelines and internship selection strategies.

2. Includes the latest APPIC rules governing internship selection and explains how they affect applicants.

3. Helps you determine your professional and personal priorities and use these factors to determine what internships will best meet your needs.

4. Teaches you how to locate and evaluate internships that fulfill your personal priorities.

5. Describes how you can determine the competitiveness of various programs and lists the programs receiving the most applications.

6. Discloses how training centers evaluate academic programs and discusses how their evaluation of your program should influence your application strategy.

7. Explains the four steps in preparing a professional resume or CV for internship applications, what to include and what to leave out, and how to organize it effectively. A sample CV is provided.

8. Advises you how to prepare effective applications, personal statements and cover letters, and how to obtain appropriate letters of recommendation.

9. Discusses traveling to internships and how to maximize your chances of arriving at your destination on time with the fewest hassles at the worst travel time of the year. Gives explicit instructions on how you can save hundreds of dollars on travel and hotel costs.

10. Describes in detail effective interviewing, including how to schedule interviews, proper dress, what to expect, and things you should and should not do during an interview or while visiting an internship. An extensive list of the questions actually asked by interviewers is provided, along with questions you should ask them.

11. Explains how to negotiate with internships honestly and effectively during the "end game" prior to "Uniform Notification Day."

12. Gives explicit instructions on what to do during Uniform Notification Day and in the days that follow.

13. Describes what to do in the event of an earthquake or some other disaster.

Shortly after Uniform Notification Day in 1991, I received a letter from Paul Bayon, a student at the Graduate School of Applied and Professional Psychology at Rutgers. Bayon wrote, "I do not know how I would have survived the horrors of the past six months without the guidance provided by your book. This volume is truly a godsend. Thank you, thank you, thank you for making this guidebook available to graduate students other than those at Florida State University! I know that it greatly helped me obtain a position at my first choice..." (Bayon, personal communication, February 13, 1991).

Bayon went on to provide a number of cogent suggestions for improving the guidebook. His comments and those of others who used the first edition of this book have been incorporated in the present revision. I hope you will find this revised and expanded edition as useful to you as the first edition was to them.

E.I.M.
Tallahassee, FL

ACKNOWLEDGEMENTS AND DEDICATION

I am grateful to many people who helped make this book and its predecessor possible. First and foremost are the many Florida State University graduate students with whom I have shared the internship application process. Their comments, encounters and reflections on their experiences form the essence of this survival guide. It is they who provided the questions in Appendices Five and Six, and the "war stories" and examples that make this book real. I especially wish to thank Mark Winiarski who wrote a detailed account of his internship application adventures as a legacy for future applicants. I also wish to thank all the applicants from other universities who wrote suggestions that helped in revising the first edition.

I am also indebted to the many internship training directors and their staffs whom I have interviewed from Los Angeles to Boston, and from Miami to Seattle, not only for their unfailing hospitality, but also for their thoughtful comments and insights on the internship selection process.

I also wish to thank the Association of Psychology Postdoctoral and Internship Programs for their contributions to both editions and for allowing me to reprint the 1991 APPIC rules in Appendix One. In particular I wish to thank Bernhard Blom, Robert Klepac and Sanford Peterson for their advice regarding computer matching and other aspects of the selection process and Connie Hercey, APPIC's Central Office Administrator for providing back copies of the APPIC Newsletter that assisted in the revision. Sybel Russ, formerly Director of Sales for the Tallahassee office of Eastern Airlines, did her utmost to help our students travel at minimal cost, and, in the process, provided me with an education on air travel.

Both editions have benefited greatly from the infrastructure provided by George Weaver, Chair of the Psychology Department. Not only does he provide an environment conducive to scholarship, but he has also supported the extensive travel to internships around the country without which this book would not have been possible. Work on this revised edition began while I was Scholar in Residence at the Florida State University London Study Center. I wish to thank the Director, Dr. Eugene Crook, and his staff for providing me with fine facilities and opportunities for research and writing.

Debra Bonds and Sharon Wittig lent their expertise and assistance to the production of the first edition, and Sharon and Sheila Marks helped with the revision. Their good cheer and willingness to tackle difficult tasks was as helpful as their professional skills.

I also wish to thank my publisher, Dr. Joe Hollis, for taking a chance and publishing an unconventional book for a specialized readership. If you find this book helpful, thank him for bringing it to you.

Most of all I wish to acknowledge the contribution of my wife, Sara Jill Mercer. While I worked on this revision, she took care of our move from London back to the US, and saw to the sale of one house and the purchase of another. Once the first draft was complete, she did the copy editing and then produced the manuscript in camera-ready form, just as she had done with the first edition. She was my partner and collaborator on all phases of this enterprise, as she is on everything worthwhile in my life. It is to her that this book is dedicated.

TECHNICAL NOTES

This manuscript was written on a Tandy 1500 HD laptop computer using Wordstar 5.5, and printed on a Canon BJ-10e portable bubble jet printer in NLQ PROP type. The cover illustration was drawn by the author.

CONTENTS

FOREWORD

You are embarking on one of the most challenging periods of your graduate education: selecting and striving for a predoctoral psychology internship. Most important enterprises are stressful; obtaining an internship is no exception. For some, applying for internship combines the worst aspects of seeking a mate, applying for graduate school, and taking comprehensive oral exams. On the other hand, obtaining your first full time professional position can also be challenging, exhilarating, and fulfilling. This book is designed to help minimize the strain and maximize the satisfaction.

Why do so many psychology graduate students find applying for internship so traumatic? Some apprehension is justified. Obtaining a good internship is important for your career, and it is essential that you do it right the first time. An applicant who does not experience any anxiety probably does not understand the situation or is not especially serious about a career in professional psychology.

However, a great deal of your trepidation is unnecessary. Some of it stems from fear of the unknown. You are applying for a professional psychology internship and you do not know what to expect or how to go about it. Relax. This book will tell you all you need to know. Other worries are caused by your irrational beliefs. In the course of your professional training you have undoubtedly counseled clients to put aside their unrealistic expectations so they can concentrate on coping effectively with more realistic concerns. Now it is time to heed your own counsel. Let us begin by exorcising some of the demons that seem to haunt many intern applicants.

1

OBTAINING A PSYCHOLOGY INTERNSHIP

Some unrealistic worries

Procuring the perfect internship. Many internship applicants operate under the illusion that somewhere there exists the one perfect program that is ideal for them and that their careers will be ruined if they do not procure a position there. Some are even convinced that there is a single special slot or rotation within that ideal internship that they must seek and obtain. This is utter nonsense. There are currently about 500 clinical internships listed by the Association of Psychology Postdoctoral and Internship Centers ("APPIC") (APPIC, 1991b). Unless your needs are very unusual, many, probably most, of these sites would meet your basic training needs. At the same time, it is extremely unlikely that any of the 500 would meet all your needs perfectly. So, although your decision is an important one, try not to get too obsessive about it.

After reading the above, you probably nodded and proceeded to this paragraph secure in the knowledge that my admonition not to seek the perfect placement as if it was the Holy Grail does not apply to you. You are much too sophisticated and professional to subscribe to such a naive belief. Wonderful. Just remember your sophistication and professionalism the week before Notification Day if you are starting to panic over the possibility that you might not get into your first choice program.

Evaluation anxiety. Internship applications involve evaluations, and this makes some people nervous. As a psychologist, you are going to be making appraisals every day of your professional career. Whether it is in a formal assessment, a therapeutic interaction, a consultation with another professional, or a supervisory session, you are constantly evaluating other people, and they in turn are examining you.

The same thing happens when you are applying for internship. You will be sizing up the program and staff and at the same time they will be evaluating you. If you think of the internship interview as just another professional assessment, your anxiety should decrease.

Competition anxiety. Many students get scared by the numbers. According to a recent report (APPIC, 1991b), there are about 12 applications submitted for every fully funded APA-accredited internship position. Before you panic, you must remember that this is the number of applications, not applicants. The average student applies to 14 places (Eggert Laughlin, Hutzell, Stedman, Solway & Carrington, 1987) and some to twice that many. Even a "superstar" who receives offers from a number of programs can occupy only one position. Moreover, there is a great disparity in the numbers of students applying to various facilities. Data that I extracted from the Directory of Internship and Postdoctoral Programs in Professional Psychology (APPIC, 1991a) show that there were 41 internship centers that each received 100 or more applications. Although they constituted only eight percent of the total, these popular programs accounted for almost 25% of the total number of applications. The remaining 92% are obviously less competitive.

Later in this book I shall go into more detail on assessing the competitiveness of various internships and how to decide how many applications you should submit. In the interim, you may find it reassuring to learn that a number of internship program directors recently conducted a survey to answer the question, "Is the supply of APIC-member intern positions...outstripping the demand for them by clinical, counseling and school psychology students?" (Stedman, Costello, Gaines, Solway, Zimet and Carrington (1990, p. 37). So while you are worrying that there may be too many applicants and not enough positions, the internships are stewing over whether there are too many slots for the available number of candidates.

Fear of rejection. A third irrational fear is that of experiencing rejection. You may as well accept the fact right now that you will be rejected. No matter how fabulous you are, it is unlikely that every setting you visit will decide that you are a good match for their program. I know of one program that passed over an applicant because they felt he was too good; even though this program is highly competitive, they felt he was so good he would probably go to one that was even more prestigious. We will have more to say about this sort of second guessing later. Another candidate was a brilliant researcher, a gifted clinician and fluent in two languages. Most training programs pursued her as if she was the graduate student equivalent of a Heisman Trophy winner. However, even this paragon did not get accepted everywhere. One program turned her down because they felt she was far too attractive: "The head nurse would have killed me if I brought her in here," the Training Director later confessed.

If these two candidates could get rejected, so can you. But relax; you will soon discover that you do not like every program you apply to. Some will not meet your needs; others will simply not appeal to you. So why should you expect every program to fancy having you as a trainee? Such rejections, often mutual, are inevitable. Worrying about them is a waste of time.

Some realistic concerns

Once you stop stewing over irrational worries, you can deal more effectively with the realistic difficulties applying for internship poses. Virtually all of these problems can be anticipated. If you prepare for them, you will be able to cope with them more successfully.

Applying is a hassle. I am afraid that this is a legitimate concern. Fox (1991, p.34) describes the present process as "disruptive to the lives of our students," and, indeed, applying for internship will come to dominate your life in the months to come. Identifying the training centers that will best meet your particular needs, filling out application forms, preparing a Curriculum Vitae ("CV"), traveling to the sites, interviewing and negotiating with training centers will require a lot of time and effort. I will tell you what to do and how to do it, but it will be up to you to get the job done correctly and on time.

Applying takes too much time. This is also true, so in planning your schedule for the year you apply be sure to budget adequate time for the internship application process. Figure on it requiring at least as much time as the most rigorous graduate course you have ever taken and modify your academic schedule accordingly.

Applying is expensive. Costs are another realistic consideration. The Dean of a school of professional psychology recently noted, "Going for interviews... creates real financial hardships for most students...It is not unusual for our students to have expenses of $2,000 in interview costs alone" (Fox, 1991, p. 34). If you follow the advice in this book, you will save hundreds of dollars. Nevertheless, you should be prepared for substantial extra expenditures for travel, telephone, and wardrobe additions.

Impact of your decision. Another realistic concern is that selecting an internship is an important professional decision that will significantly influence your career. The skills you develop and the techniques you learn will stay with you throughout your career, and the professional relationships you develop and contacts you make will have a major influence on your subsequent opportunities. Choosing an internship is an important task that deserves your serious attention.

Fear of the unknown

A major source of anxiety for everyone involved in the internship selection process, Internship Training Directors ("TD"s) and University Directors of Clinical Training ("DCT"s) as well as students, is loss of control. No one can predict exactly what will happen, and no one can control the outcome.

For applicants, this lack of control is compounded by not knowing exactly what is involved in the internship selection process. While your university or professional school training program may have provided you with excellent academic training, few prepare you for the process of finding and obtaining an appropriate internship. You can be forgiven if you feel like Alice playing croquet with the Queen of Hearts. Until you understand the process, it is like playing a game on someone else's field with whimsical rules that often appear arbitrary, if indeed they are ever articulated. True, APPIC has published a formal set of explicit regulations, but at times these are incidental to what is actually happening.

I can appreciate your bewilderment. When I first assumed the role of Director of Clinical Training ("DCT") at the Florida State University, I suddenly realized I knew virtually nothing about internship selection and training. Like most line faculty, I had concerned myself with the academic preparation of my students and let the previous DCTs handle all the details of internships.

Being a clinical psychologist, I can understand and deal with people better if I have met them face to face. So I set out to meet the Training Directors and their faculties by personally visiting the various internships our students were attending around the country, a practice I have continued ever since. These visits are good for our students' morale and allow me to evaluate their progress, but they also help me to learn about the various training programs first hand. I ask the internship personnel how they select students, what they look for in a candidate and what turns them off. The more I know about their programs and procedures, the better I can advise applicants. Other valuable information can be obtained from students who are currently on internship and at the annual meeting of APPIC, which is open to the public.

I soon discovered that predoctoral psychology internship selection is a truly unique process. It differs from the procedures used in medical schools and from every other selection system that I have encountered. It has its own arcane beliefs and rules, most of which were unwritten prior to the publication of this book. And, of course, each participant's perception of the process is somewhat different.

Several years ago, to assist our students who were applying for internship, I prepared a guidebook to explain these selection procedures and suggest successful strategies they could use. We began having regular meetings of the internship applicants at which we discussed various topics relevant to applying for internship, including ethical issues, suggestions on preparing a CV, tips on travel and advice on how to interview. These discussions were enriched by my students' reports of their adventures and by my personal experiences as I traveled from Miami to Seattle and from Boston to Los Angeles visiting our interns and meeting their supervisors and friends. As this material was incorporated into the guidebook it grew larger and more cumbersome. Nevertheless, I began to receive requests for copies from students and DCTs at other universities.

Going to the copying center to purchase copies for students in other programs soon became tedious. Moreover, much of the material in the guidebook was specific to our program. Eventually I decided to write a general book on obtaining a psychology internship, and Dr. Joe Hollis of Accelerated Development agreed to take a chance and publish it. In it I included material from the class handouts and guidebooks as well as other information, such as the politics of intern selection, that I had previously just discussed in class sessions. Appendices were added to provide a sample CV and interview questions applicants could review. I even drew a picture for the cover! When Accelerated Development displayed the first copy at the 1990 APA Convention in Boston, it had twice as much information in a compact paperback that could be conveniently carried on the road. Not only was it less bulky than the old Xeroxed guidebook, but it cost only half as much.

In the two years since the first edition was published there have been important changes in the selection process. Computerized matching of applicants with placements, a topic that occupied considerable space in the first edition, was tested and abandoned. Instead, a revised set of regulations that are more stringent and detailed than any previous rules was adopted. New data on the number of internships and the competitiveness of various setting are now available. Two classes of intern applicants have used the book and provided feedback and suggestions for improvement. This revised and expanded edition of A Guide to Obtaining a Psychology Internship incorporates all of this material. (I even drew a new picture for the cover; to please those who objected that the first edition had a man standing while a woman typed their resumes, this time the woman is standing while the man is doing the typing. I even gave her a perm and a new outfit!)

Plan for this volume

The first chapter of this book describes the politics of intern selection. One reason why the rules have changed so often is that different procedures give different groups ...the TDs, the DCTs and the applicants...different degrees of power. If you are to make sense of the internship selection process and cope with it successfully, it is essential that you understand the concerns and vested interests of the other parties and how their power struggles have influenced the selection process over the years.

After this introduction, Chapter Two will give you an overview and timetable of what you must do to identify the internships that best meet your needs and prepare successful applications. The succeeding chapters will expand on these points.

Your first task is deciding where to apply. Chapter Three helps you formulate the priorities you will use in choosing internships, and Chapter Four will advise you on how to obtain accurate information about the internships that interest you.

The next two chapters deal with the application process. Chapter Five will instruct you on how to prepare a resume or CV specifically for internship applications, and Chapter Six gives you advice on submitting the other forms and what you should and should not include.

Once your applications are all in, you should visit as many of the internship sites as you can. Chapter Seven gives you advice on travel, especially on how to reduce transportation and hotel costs. Chapter Eight deals with interviewing, as does Appendices Five and Six.

By January, most of the interviewing is over. This is when the "Endgame" begins as applicants and TDs dance elaborate minuets and attempt to second guess each other. Chapter Nine tells you what to do during the Endgame. It also provides explicit instructions on what you should do on Notification Day. It concludes with a discussion of what to do if disaster strikes.

This book is designed to help you with all phases of obtaining your internship. To get started, I suggest that you read the first two chapters and then skim over the rest of the book to give yourself an overview of what you need to do. Don't forget to examine the Appendices; they are included to help you. Later, reread each chapter from "Establishing Priorities" to "The Endgame" more closely when it is time for you to deal with each of the tasks described. You can use the timetable in Chapter Two to keep on schedule.

CHAPTER ONE:

THE POLITICS OF INTERN SELECTION

You will find that applying for an internship in professional psychology is unlike anything you have previously experienced. At first, the process will resemble applying to college or graduate school. The paperwork required is much the same, and your anxieties will be similar. But you will soon discover that applying for internship is different. When you call programs to inquire about the status of your application or innocently ask how things look, some may respond like CIA agents being interviewed by Mike Wallace, saying that they are not allowed to provide such information. When you ask for interviews, you may find that some places do not allow interviews and that others interview only those whom they invite. During the interviews themselves, you may be asked personal or probing questions unlike those you have experienced in previous employment interviews. Finally, unlike your previous experiences with college and graduate school, you may be subjected to considerable pressure to make a decision and commit yourself to your first choice.

At first, you might worry that there is something about you that is making these people nervous. Did your major professor actually write the awful letter she threatened to send? Did you suffer a major deodorant failure while interviewing? If you keep these things to yourself, you will suffer needless anxieties; when you share your experiences with other applicants, you will soon discover that they are having similar experiences.

After it is over, many applicants liken the internship application process to dating and courtship. The comparison is apt. As in dating, there is a period of mild flirtation that gets more intense

11

as certain relationships get more serious, and, as in courtship, there is the question of which party should risk rejection by making the first commitment. For the Internship Training Directors in particular, there is also the constant fear of being left at the altar. But unless you have had the experience of managing several serious relationships simultaneously, knowing that you will soon have to commit yourself to one and only one, you have not had an adequate foretaste of the internship application experience.

Politics and poker

The reason you will find applying for internships unique is that, unlike college admissions or courtships, the internship selection process is basically political... political in the sense that it involves negotiation, compromise and a delicate balance of power relationships. The balance of power has changed over the years, and it will continue to change as the rules continue to be modified.

The principal players in this political poker game are 1) the internship Training Director(s) ("TDs"), 2) the university Directors of Clinical Training ("DCTs") and you, the graduate students who are applying for internship. Among the secondary players are the staffs at the internship sites, including the current interns, your major professor and other interested faculty members, your fellow graduate students, some of whom may have a vested interest in whether or not you are accepted at a certain site, and friends or family members whose lives will be affected by your choice of internship. Correctly or not, all the players perceive this as a high stakes game in which their careers may be on the line; this perception generates considerable stress and tension for all involved.

This poker game has been going on annually since 1949, the date of the first Boulder Conference on professional training in psychology.

Before you ante up and take a hand, you should get acquainted with the other players and learn what has been happening in the game so far. To play your hand effectively, you first need to understand the other players' goals, what it is they hope to accomplish if they succeed, and what it is they fear will happen if they fail. These hopes and fears are the keys to their game plans and the reason why different groups keep tinkering with the house rules in the hope of gaining an advantage over the others. The better your understanding of the game and its players, the more of an edge you will have.

The legacy of the Boulder Conference

Professional psychology as we know it today was established at the Boulder (Colorado) Conference in 1949. At that conference, several decisions were made that permanently shaped the nature of our graduate training:

1. The doctoral degree was established as the minimum educational standard for the independent practice of professional psychology.

2. All professional psychologists were to be trained as scientists as well as professionals.

3. In order to implement the scientist-professional model, graduate students would receive academic training in a university setting. There they would learn core concepts of psychology and, through a combination of course work, practica and research, clinical psychologists would be trained in research, assessment, and psychotherapy.

4. A one year internship in a recognized clinical setting was required before the professional degree would be granted (Sundberg, Taplin, & Tyler, 1983, p. 19).

Thus, from the very beginning, graduate training in psychology has involved three groups

13

with somewhat different concerns and interests: the university and professional school faculties, the internship centers and the students. In this chapter we will focus on the first two groups because it is they who are involved in internship selection year after year and who have had the primary role in establishing and monitoring the selection procedures. (Don't worry; the rest of the book will focus on applicants and their concerns.)

The first group consists of the Directors of Clinical Training and the other faculty members at the degree-granting institutions. As you well know, this is hardly a monolithic group. Programs differ greatly in the emphasis they place on professional training, and within each school individual faculty members often have different attitudes and opinions regarding what you should look for in an internship. Your clinical supervisor might recommend a program with a certain theoretical orientation. Your major professor may be more concerned with whether your internship will afford you time to complete your dissertation research. Your DCT may urge you to apply to a program with which your university has strong historic ties.

In the two decades following the Boulder Conference, the university faculties held the bulk of the power in deciding clinical training issues. Many graduate students were supported by USPHS Predoctoral Fellowships which were controlled and distributed by the faculty. Others were supported by faculty members' research grants, which were also plentiful during the days of the Great Society. Driven by the need to educate the "baby boom" population which was enrolling in colleges and universities during the 1960s, academic departments were expanding and proliferating, providing a ready source of employment opportunities for research-oriented clinical psychologists.

When the academic departments held sway, the university-based Directors of Clinical Training and the major professors had a major role in placing students in internships. Successful DCTs established networks of training facilities, often staffed by former students, which could be relied upon to accept the students they recommended. Some major professors had similar relationships with certain training centers, albeit on a smaller scale. A student working with "Prof. Salmon Kingfish," for example, could expect to intern at the "Halibut Hospital" where Kingfish's prize graduate, "Dr. Almondine Dover-Sole," was Training Director. By the same token, cooperative Training Directors such as Dover-Sole could count on regularly getting well qualified students from these universities. The students had little to say about where they went, but they also did not have to go through all the hassle today's students must endure.

Nowadays, except for the DCT, most university faculty members are much less involved in internship applications than they were when the "Old Boy" networks were more influential. There are many reasons for the decline in faculty influence, interest, and participation. They include the decrease in the number of academic and research positions available for new Ph.D.s, the phasing out of federally-funded clinical training grants along with the increasing competition for research grants, the resulting increase in the proportion of professionally-trained psychologists seeking positions in applied rather than academic settings, and the entry of large numbers of young "baby boomers" into the profession which has served to dilute the "Old Boy's" influence.

Although they are less obvious now than they were in the past, networks still exist. DCTs who take an active role in placing interns from their programs establish good working relationships with the TDs at the internships their students frequently attend. These relationships facilitate the exchange of information on students' progress during the internship year. They are also invaluable in sorting things out during internship selection. If your DCT does not play an

15

active role, do not despair. Most students nowadays work things out on their own. But a DCT who is familiar with the various internships and their programs and knows the training personnel at the agencies can be very helpful during the application process.

It would be a mistake to assume the old networks have totally disappeared. Instead they are dormant, but sometimes they show unexpected signs of life. After interviewing, a student was very impressed with the program at the "Moosehead Medical Center." In fact, it was her first choice. I noticed that the student had once taken a practicum with "Prof. Muledeer," one of our senior faculty, and that the Moosehead training program was headed by "Dr. Carry Boux," who years before had had Prof. Muledeer as her major professor. I suggested that the student ask Prof. Muledeer if he would call Dr. Boux and put in a good word for her. Two days later I was astounded to receive a note from Prof. Muledeer saying that the student had been accepted at Moosehead Medical; Selection Day was still a month away.

Incidents like these are becoming increasingly rare, however. Today, once university faculty members have written their letters of recommendation, they rarely get involved in the internship application process. As travel funds have become increasingly scarce, it has become difficult even for the DCTs, whose job it is to monitor their students' professional training, to visit the internships where their students are training.

With the university faculty largely out of the picture, the principle players left in the intern selection process are the training center personnel and the applicants. Interestingly, each fears the other and feels the other has too much control over the final outcome of the selection process. The result has been a continual tinkering with the rules for notification of candidates and shifts back and forth in the balance of power.

As a graduate student about to apply for internship it may seem strange that Training Directors may feel that you are too powerful and have too much control over the final outcome. Nevertheless, it is true, and until you understand their fears you will not be able to fathom their behavior. Let us see how this odd state of affairs came about.

The emergence of APPIC and Uniform Notification

The current rules governing the internship selection and notification process were formulated and established by "APIC," the Association of Psychology Internship Centers, now known as APPIC, the Association of Psychology Postdoctoral and Internship Centers. (For the sake of simplicity, I will use the current acronym throughout.) The internship training centers formed the association in the 1970s in an attempt to regulate the unbridled competition among rival training programs which was making a shambles of the internship selection process, causing undue hardship for students and agencies alike (Fox, 1990). Its' first and greatest achievement was getting all the various internships to agree on a common day when offers would be made. This is sometimes referred to as "Uniform Notification Day" and sometimes as "Selection Day." Training Directors refer to it as "Intern Calling Day." All these terms are interchangeable.

Although students and DCTs tend to regard APPIC as a massive, monolithic force, probably because APPIC unilaterally establishes the rules, in reality it has been a poorly funded loose confederation that literally lived out of a cardboard box, "... a traveling road show, moving from one location to another with each new election" (Stedman, 1989, p. 35). Producing the Directory each year strained its resources, and only recently was APPIC able to establish a one-secretary central office. The organization has little real power, and must rely on the cooperation and voluntary compliance of its members.

17

Aside from moral persuasion, APPIC has no real authority to investigate complaints or levy meaningful sanctions. In view of these limitations, the organization has been remarkably successful in bringing some semblance of order to a chaotic process.

Although the "Old Boy" system had worked well for the Old Boys, by the late 1960s and early 1970s there was an increasing number of New Boys, and New Girls as well, who wanted a piece of the action. Moreover, the lack of common ground rules in the intern selection process could put students in difficult, even intolerable, situations.

Imagine yourself as a student in the days before APPIC. If you had a well-connected DCT or major professor, like Prof. Kingfish or Prof. Muledeer, you attended the internship your mentor arranged for you. Otherwise you went through an application process similar to the current one. Of course, there was no APPIC Directory then, so you relied on the brochures sent by the various facilities. Let us suppose that after reading the brochures, interviewing at the various sites and discussing them with faculty and friends, you decided that the best internship site for you was the "Codliver Consortium" and that your second choice was the "Septicemia School of Medicine."

In the days before APPIC and Uniform Notification you might have received a call from the Training Director at Septicemia in mid-January offering you an internship for the coming year and giving you 48 hours in which to decide, after which the offer would be withdrawn. You, or your DCT, would then call the Training Director at Codliver and discover that they were operating on a different schedule and were still actively interviewing applicants. While they had been very impressed with you and your credentials and considered you definitely in the running, no offers would be made to anyone until February.

Assuming your DCT could not cut some deal with the Codliver TD or get the people at Septicemia to back off, you would be left with two options: 1) you could accept the position at Septicemia and make a binding commitment to attend their program, or 2) you could decline and hope that you would get an offer from Codliver. (Don't even think about the possibility of accepting Septicemia and changing your mind if you subsequently got a Codliver offer. One thing that has remained constant in the internship game is that anyone who reneges on an internship commitment is doomed.)

In his recent history of the Association, Stedman (1989, p. 35) wrote, "APIC was organized primarily to deal with a lack of regularity in the intern selection process ... students of the late '60s complained about deals being made between internship sites and certain select students... [They]... complained that their clinical training directors didn't know what to do [and] there was often undue stress on students."

The idea behind APPIC was that internship training centers should agree on a common set of procedures and a uniform selection schedule to eliminate unfair competition that all too often posed students with the difficult decision of whether to accept offers from their second, third or lower ranked internships before they had heard from their first choice. Under Uniform Notification, the APPIC members agreed among themselves that no Training Director could make an offer before an agreed upon time and that students were to be guaranteed a reasonable amount of time to consider these offers. Moreover, no TD could make an offer to a student who had already accepted an offer from another institution.

When this procedure was first proposed in the mid-1970s, students had five days to decide what offer to accept (Stedman, 1989, p.36). In 1976, the time was reduced to three days, and by 1989 applicants had at most 28 hours to respond.

The latest revision of the rules provides students with a maximum of seven hours. As of 1992, no formal offers can be made until 9:00 AM, Central Standard Time, on the second Monday in February, and students have until 4:00 PM, CST the same day to accept or reject the offer. After 4:00 PM CST, the offer is automatically rescinded. Of course, if a student doesn't receive a call until 3:58 PM Monday, that does not leave a whole lot of time for reflection. This is why it is essential to rank all the places to which you have applied before Notification Day.

In the interests of fairness to applicants and internship training centers alike, APPIC also stipulates that no training center can make more offers than they have slots available. Each internship has a limited number of funded positions which they feel it is vitally important to fill. Once an offer has been made to an applicant, that opening is regarded as committed and, until the applicant declines the offer, it is unavailable and cannot be offered to anyone else. In short, a student who is holding an offer owns that slot until the selection period ends. An agency with 6 positions cannot make 8 offers figuring two people will probably decline. Once the sixth position has been offered, the TD is out of business. It is this rule that differentiates internship selection from college and graduate school admissions.

Every Training Director knows of cases in which students for various reasons have held offers for what appear to be excessive periods of time. Some may be unable to decide. This can occur when a couple is trying to make a joint decision, but as one intern applicant noted, "Some students will begin the day without knowing how they will respond if offered a particular internship" (Jacob, 1987, p. 154). Of course the principle reason students hold offers is because they are waiting for an offer from another institution they would prefer to attend.

In order to protect themselves, an intern-

ship with offers outstanding will urge the applicants on its alternate list not to accept another
position until the agency has received definite
responses of acceptance or rejection to all the bids
that are being held. Indeed, it will probably try
to maintain two or three viable alternates for
every unresolved position. If the alternates agree
to wait, they will naturally hold on to the offers
they may have received from their lower ranked
internships, which in turn will ask their alternates
not to accept other offers and so the problem is
compounded.

Sometimes a gridlock may occur in one
segment of the system (May & Dana, 1990).
Student A may have internship X for a first
choice and Y as his second, while student B has
Y as her first choice and X as the second. Let us
suppose that at 9:00 AM, internship X offers a
slot to B, while Y chooses student A. Both students decide to hold on to these offers hoping to
get accepted at their first choice institutions,
and indeed program X calls applicant A, and facility Y calls candidate B, assuring them they are
first alternates and will receive an offer as soon
as an opening becomes available. Since the internships cannot withdraw offers once made, this
deadlock can continue until A or B decides to
accept their second choice or until the 4:00 PM
deadline arrives. I was told of a three-way gridlock which was resolved only after one of the TDs
involved correctly diagnosed the stalemate, called
the other two TDs, and worked out a compromise
whereby all three institutions agreed to settle for
their second choice candidates, thereby giving the
applicants their first choice placements. This
initiative was no doubt a violation of some rule,
but in this case it worked in the students' favor.

As the number of applicants and internship
positions increases, the chances of a gridlock
occurring become increasingly improbable. The
greatest risk is in some small subset of the system
as, for example, several candidates competing for
a few highly specialized positions. However,

the mere possibility that such an event can occur illustrates a flaw in the Uniform Notification system.

The Training Director's dilemma

Let us look at Uniform Notification Day from the viewpoint of Dr. "Epi Glottis," the Director of Internship Training at the "Eastern Esophagus Internship Consortium." Eastern Esophagus has six slots which Epi's boss, Chief Psychologist "Chester Sternum," wants filled with hardworking, brilliant, congenial interns from the nation's most prestigious universities, stratified to represent all the major ethnic groups and most of the typical genders. Dr. Sternum expects that they will all go on to achieve great success which they will attribute to the magnificent training they received at Eastern Esophagus. Dr. Glottis shares these aspirations, but will settle for filling all six slots with competent students who are reasonably free of psychopathology and will not precipitate any major lawsuits in the course of training.

If Dr. Glottis' fondest hopes are realized, this is how Notification Day will proceed. Over the weekend, Dr. Glottis and the admissions staff have ranked all the applicants, taking into account their qualifications and abilities as well as the likelihood that they will accept an offer. (More about the importance of this latter criterion later.) At 9:00 AM, Central Time, on Notification Day, Dr. Glottis calls the first-ranked applicant who promptly accepts. At 9:01 the second call goes out with the same results. By 9:06, all six slots have been filled with the six top ranked applicants. At 9:07, Dr. Glottis wonders briefly if they should have made an offer to the superstar that they put on the alternate list because it seemed likely she would go elsewhere. Deciding not to worry over what might have been, Epi notifies Dr. Sternum that they have signed up all their top applicants, tells a subordinate to notify the alternates that Esophagus has filled all its slots, turns off the phone, and begins working on the quarterly evaluations of the current interns which have been neglected during selection season.

What would a bad day be like? Contrary to what you might suppose, a truly bad day is not one in which one or more of the top candidates reject their offers. When this happens, Dr. Glottis can usually fill the six slots with applicants on the alternate list; indeed, Epi might be pleasantly surprised when the superstar accepts. No, a truly bad day occurs when one or more candidates inform Dr. Glottis that they will neither accept or reject but "hold" the offer. If this occurs, Dr. Glottis will quickly start calling the lower ranked applicants to inform them they are high on the alternate list, assure them that there is a good chance a slot will open up shortly, and ask them not to accept any offers until they have heard from Esophagus. The rest of the day will be spent massaging the alternates and asking the students who are holding offers when they will be able to decide. Some may simply be having difficulty deciding where to go, but most will be on the alternate lists of other institutions that they would prefer to attend but which have offers out to other applicants who are waiting to hear from someone else and so on.

Meanwhile, Dr. Glottis' list of alternate applicants may be melting away like a snowball in a pizza oven. If a candidate takes a long time to reject an offer, most of the applicants on the alternate list may accept other positions. Esophagus will be unlikely to get the exact mix of interns they wanted and may even be unable to fill all their slots. Failure to fill positions can cause serious problems for an internship training center. Positions not filled may be swept in the next budget; commitments to faculty members or agencies to provide students for a certain specific rotations may have to be revoked.

As Notification Day proceeds, some uncommitted students may be amazed to receive offers from internships that earlier refused to grant them interviews or notified them they were no longer under consideration. DCTs at major universities start getting calls from TDs at internships that have failed to fill all their slots, asking if they have any students who are still uncommitted. If so, these TDs sometimes indicate they are willing to accept them on the DCTs' recommendation, sight unseen, so eager are they to achieve their quotas.

Given this background, you can see why many, perhaps most, Training Directors feel the Uniform Notification system places too much power in the hands of students. Two coping strategies have resulted. One, which we might call the "knowledge is power" strategy, is to make offers only to applicants who are certain to accept. The other is to change the house rules to make the game less risky for the internship centers. We will discuss each.

Knowledge is power

In a real poker game, all the players reveal their cards at the same time. However, on Notification Day, the internships have to show their hands, but the students can continue to play while keeping their cards concealed. No wonder many TDs feel this is unfair. No wonder they would like to "peek at your hand" to find out how you will respond if they make you an offer. Training centers know they can minimize the risk by making offers only to candidates they can rely on to accept their bids.

In the "Old Days," before APPIC, internships could make an offer whenever they chose, and withdraw it if the applicant did not accept immediately. Or they would ask an applicant, "If we make you an offer, will you accept?" Under the APPIC rules, which are included in every internship's brochure, this is no longer permissible. Rule 3 states, "No internship offers in any form may be extended by agencies before the beginning of selection day," and section "c" further states, "Internship programs may not solicit information regarding an applicant's ranking of programs or his/her intention to accept or decline an offer of admission until after that offer is officially tendered." (See Appendix One.)

Rules or no rules, as Notification Day approaches, applicants discover that many, perhaps most, of the programs to which they applied try to determine whether or not they are likely to accept an offer if it is made. Some wait for candidates to call them after interviewing, and then ask them if they need any more information in order to reach a decision. This quickly leads to a subtle or not so subtle inquiry as to what the nature of the decision is likely to be. If applicants don't call, some internships infer they are not interested. Others take the initiative and call the candidates directly to see "how things are going." Some may call the DCT or major professor.

This puts students in a dilemma. How much should they reveal? Will disclosing the obvious fact that nine of the 10 internships to which they have applied are not ranked first ruin their chances for acceptance if their first choice does not come through with an offer? In response to this pressure, many call their top-ranked institutions to find out how they stand. This puts the TDs into a bind because APPIC Rule 2-b states, "No other information (such as the agency's ranking of the applicant; status as alternate/first choice, etc.) may be communicated to applicants prior to selection day." Some finesse the problem by discussing the student's status with the DCT. Others refuse to impart any information to anyone, including whether a candidate is still under active consideration, even though this is supposed to be required. Not surprisingly, no one, TDs, DCTs or students, has been satisfied with this system, so there have been a number of efforts to seek a better solution.

Changes in the selection procedures

Early notification. If internship Selection Committees could be sure that their offers would be accepted, most of their risks would be eliminated, at least insofar as the agencies are concerned. In 1986/87 this led APPIC to adopt a procedure known as "Early Notification." Two weeks before Uniform Notification Day, students who chose to participate were allowed to notify one and only one internship that they would accept an offer if it was made. This commitment was binding on those applicants. The TDs had one day to survey the pool of applicants who had made these unilateral commitments and select as many as they liked. The next day they notified these applicants that they were accepted; those who were not chosen took part in the regular Uniform Notification procedure the following week.

Early Notification provided the internship Training Directors with a no-risk pool of committed applicants who would definitely accept an offer. Not surprisingly, many of the best internships filled on Early Acceptance Day, leaving the applicants who had not been chosen or who chose not to participate to scramble for the remaining slots at less desirable agencies on the regular Notification Day.

From the standpoint of many Training Directors, especially those at the most popular programs, Early Notification was wonderful because it removed all the uncertainty from the selection process. However, from the standpoint of the applicants who had to decide whether to participate and then had only one chance to make a unilateral, binding commitment, Early Notification was extremely anxiety provoking. There was a great deal of second guessing, and some students chose to make early commitments to less prestigious second or even third choice programs where they felt they had a better chance of being chosen. In the Fall of 1988, by a narrow margin, APPIC voted to discontinue Early Notification.

Computer matching

The major drawback to both Early Notification and Uniform Notification is that both required sequential commitments. In Early Notification, based on the limited information they had available, the candidates had to make binding commitments to the programs. In Uniform Notification, it is the training centers that must make binding commitments to applicants. Under either system, the party making the offer is relatively helpless and must wait while the other party decides whether or not to accept.

Under Uniform Notification, as in a poker game, it is to each player's advantage to know what is in the other player's hand. Internships would like to know which applicants will accept their offers, and candidates want to know how they stand with the internships. This is what drives all the phone calls and manipulations during the final phases of internship selection. In particular, training centers often attempt to get candidates to make commitments or at least indicate their choices prior to Notification Day (Zimet, 1991). When the training center is the candidate's first choice, there is no problem. But if not, simply stalling for time indicates to the training center that they are not ranked first and may make them hesitate to make an offer on Notification Day.

For many years it had been suggested that these disparities could be avoided if everyone made their decisions privately and then communicated them simultaneously, as in a real poker game. This would eliminate the problems of "stalling," "holding," and "stringing along" that have plagued the Uniform Notification process. Computerized matching is simply a simultaneous examination of the choices made by the candidates and the training centers seeking the optimal fit. (It should be noted it is not essential to employ a computer in the process. However, without a computer it would involve weeks instead of hours and the likelihood of errors would be vastly greater.)

In the late 1980s, APPIC seriously considered adopting computerized matching. Proponents argued that computer matching had been used for years in medical internship selection, and that it would free applicants and programs alike to rank their choices on their merits without worrying about how their choices were ranking them. Not only would this remove most of the second guessing and skullduggery from the selection process, but it would also eliminate the time, stress and expense that accompany National Notification Day. Opponents feared losing control, and argued that software programs could not deal with contingent choices, such as, "If my spouse gets an internship at the Southwest Schizophrenia Center, I would want to go to Arizona Anorexia, but if my partner is going to New England Neuropathology, I would prefer to attend Boston Bulimia."

A special APPIC committee developed a matching program that was tested in a nationwide pilot study during the 1989/90 internship selection process. The question was whether the hypothetical computer match would come up with assignments that were as satisfactory or better than those obtained using the regular Uniform Notification procedure. Since the program was based on the assumption that 100% of the sites and applicants would participate, as would be the case if it was adopted, it was not designed to deal with missing data. Unfortunately, 15% of the internships, 5% of the university programs and an unknown proportion of the individual applicants did not participate. As the committee noted, "We sadly realized that, inevitably, incomplete data produce incomplete and inconclusive results" (Blom, Pederson & Klepac, 1990, p. 20). Following this trial run, APPIC held a referendum on whether or not computer matching should be adopted; it was defeated by a vote of 183 against to 141 in favor.

For the foreseeable future it appears likely

that APPIC will remain with Uniform Notification. Some day, computer matching may be tried again. If so, it is likely that it will be mandatory rather than elective. Following the 1990 referendum, Zimet, who was then the Chair of APPIC wrote, "As long as we have a non-binding trial, there will be programs that will choose not to participate and we shall never know the real outcome...If in the future another effort is made to set up a computer match, it is my opinion that the computer matching decision must be the one that counts. If it were done that way, no program could afford not to participate for the internships would get no trainees and the University programs could not place their students" (1990, p. 4).

If computer matching is again attempted, here is what will happen. After you have completed all your applications and gone on your interviews, when the time comes to make your selections you will be given a form on which to rank order those internships you applied to which you are willing to attend. You will then send the form to APPIC along with a signed statement that you will abide by the results. The selection algorithm is designed in such a way that your best chance to get the internship of your choice is to rank your choices in exactly the preferred order. If you applied to some dream internship that you would love to attend but fear you have no realistic chance of obtaining, go ahead and put it first. You have absolutely nothing to lose. If they listed you sufficiently high, you will get the match; if your "dream internship," or even several dream internships, did not rank you high enough for you to be matched there, the program will proceed on to your next choices. You have nothing to lose and everything to gain by calling it exactly as you see it.

On some specified date, the forms from all the applicants and all the internships will be electronically scanned and fed into a computer. Subsequently, you will be notified, probably by letter, of the internship to which you were matched. That is where you must go if you attend any APPIC internship that year. That is why you should not list any internship you are not willing to attend. If you do not get matched with any site, you will be informed of all those places that still have openings so you can negotiate with them directly. Thus, under computer matching, the Clearinghouse is automatic and would begin immediately.

The 1991 rule changes. After computer matching was defeated, APPIC considered other ways of improving the Uniform Notification procedures. A major cause of dissatisfaction on the part of internship personnel was what they regarded as the excessive amount of time students were allowed to hold offers. As we have seen, Stedman (1989, p. 36) indicated applicants initially had five days to consider offers. This time period had been steadily reduced; by 1990/91, Notification Day began at 8:00 AM Central Standard Time on the second Monday in February and applicants had until noon the next day to respond.

This rule was changed in May, 1991. Uniform Notification now begins 9:00 AM CST and only lasts until 4:00 PM CST the same day. After 4:00 PM CST, any outstanding offer that has not been accepted is void. This does not mean that all activity ceases and uncommitted applicants go into the Clearinghouse. Internships can, if they choose, allow candidates who were holding offers more time to decide. However, they may prefer to offer those positions to candidates who have been waiting on the alternate list. The new rule also gives the alternates a definite time by which they can expect to learn whether or not they will be offered a position.

The May, 1991 revision of the rules mandated several other changes aimed at making the selection process more equitable for applicants. It is now stated that programs must notify applicants who are excluded from consideration as early as possible and no less than a week prior to Notification Day; previously the rules only stated that TDs should notify such applicants. Of course, there is no requirement that programs must exclude any applicants from consideration.

The new rules also state that, once a center has filled all its positions, it must notify all the remaining applicants who have not been selected and who have not notified the agency they have accepted positions elsewhere, by phone as soon as possible. Those that cannot be reached by phone must be sent a letter within 72 hours. The previous rules only said that the internship should notify the remaining applicants, and did not specify that it should be done promptly. Many did not bother to do so, and others simply sent out form letters several days later.

Finally, the May, 1991 revision includes a new rule stating that training centers should document the verbal agreement with each applicant in a letter specifying the terms and conditions of the appointment, such as the stipend, fringe benefits and starting date. From a legal standpoint, this can be extremely important. Several internship programs had their funding withdrawn or frozen during the 1991 recession; the acceptance letters which had been mailed out were important evidence that a binding commitment had been made to the trainees (Larsen, 1991). It is for this reason that I recommend that applicants specify their understanding of the terms of employment when they send their acceptance letters to the internship.

The goals of the various players

As I noted earlier, it is essential that you understand the motives and objectives of the various players in this poker game. As an applicant, you have two basic goals. The first is obvious: obtaining an internship that meets the professional and personal needs you have defined for yourself. The second is less apparent, but also important. That is to avoid making any egregious errors that may later come back to haunt you, such as offending people who may some day be in a position to influence your career. Aside from sexually assaulting a member of the training staff, the worst error you can make is lying about your intentions. If you have assured selection personnel at an internship that their program is your first choice and you later hold or reject an offer from them, they and everyone they talk to will regard you as being untrustworthy for the rest of your career. Later in this book we will discuss how to deal with internships that press you for a commitment. You can deal with them successfully without being dishonest, and you will emerge from the internship selection process with a network of positive professional contacts as well as with the internship of your choice.

The goals of the other principal players, the Internship Training Directors and Clinical Training Directors, are less clearly defined. The TD's obvious objective is obtaining the "best" internship class possible, whatever that is. Basically it means pleasing the members of the training faculty at the internship by filling all the available slots with candidates who are ethical, reasonably competent, and free of flagrant psychopathology. The DCTs hope to place all their applicants in settings which will a) enhance the prestige of their programs, b) please the applicants' major professors, and c) provide their students with good training experiences. *in that order!*

The TDs and DCTs also have long term concerns. They play this game every year, so they must establish and maintain good professional working relations with one another. The best TDs and DCTs realize that this means being honest with one another, evaluating students and programs fairly and forthrightly.

CHAPTER TWO:

APPLYING FOR INTERNSHIP: AN OVERVIEW

Applying for internship is like planning a political campaign or a military operation. It is impossible to begin too soon or prepare too thoroughly. We begin preparing for next year's internship application season the week after Notification Day when our students who have just been selected for internships present a panel discussion describing the process and giving advice to other clinical students who will be applying in the years to come. One recent student summed up her advice in three words, "Compulse, compulse, compulse!"

There are two aspects to internship preparation. The first involves getting the academic training you need to be ready for internship. The second is preparing for the actual application process. The distinction is analogous to politics in which we differentiate governing from running for office.

Preparing for internship

The first step in applying for internship is to make sure you will be academically and professionally prepared to go on internship when the time comes. There are certain basic requirements you must meet to be eligible. The American Psychological Association's Accreditation Handbook (1986, pp. 17-18) stipulates, "The internship is taken after completion of relevant didactic and practicum work and precedes the granting of the doctoral degree." The Handbook further states that an approved graduate program must provide a minimum of 400 hours of practicum experience, at least 150 hours of which is in direct service and 75 hours in formal scheduled supervision. Intern-

33

ships can and typically do require more hours than the minimum specified by APA. The minimum number of hours each internship requires is noted in the Directory published annually by APPIC. A brief survey of the most recent Directory (APPIC, 1991a) shows requirements ranging from a low of 400 hours to a high of 2,000 hours.

Internship preparation involves more than just practicum hours, however. Your entire graduate school experience can be viewed as preparation for internship. From Day One, professional preparation, culminating in internship, is an important consideration when you choose courses and practica. Although internships vary tremendously in their orientation and expectations, most will expect you to have a thorough grounding in traditional clinical skills and to be well versed in professional ethics and behavior.

It is up to you and your advisors to determine when you will be ready for internship. In the days when the university faculties played a greater role in the internship process and most students were supported by university-based research or training grants, students often went on internship in their third or fourth year of graduate study and then returned to the university to complete the dissertation. By today's standards, the amount of clinical training some students received prior to internship was minimal. I can recall a graduate student in clinical psychology from that era who reported to internship having had courses in test construction and theories of psychotherapy, but who had never actually administered a test or counseled a client.

After the big clinical training grants were phased out during the Nixon and Ford administrations, more graduate students had to support themselves by working in clinical settings while at their universities. Practicum agencies insisted on a higher level of clinical competence if they were to pay the practicum students. As a result, by the time you go on internship it is likely you will have had more clinical experience than did your counterparts 20 years ago. I have no idea how typical our program is, but the number of practicum hours recorded by our students who applied for internship recently ranged from 1,848 to 10,257, with a mean of 5,121 hours.

One way to prepare for internship is to keep in touch with more advanced students from your academic program during their internship year, and learn from them what skills they were expected to have when they arrived. Their advice may be more salient than that of some faculty members who have not recently been actively involved in clinical work. For example, your academic courses may have made you skeptical about the validity and utility of projective tests, or you may have been taught that formal diagnosis is a sterile enterprise. Nevertheless, on internship you better be prepared to come up with a formal diagnosis according to the latest nomenclature and be able to administer, score and interpret traditional psychometric instruments such as the Rorschach.

A number of academic considerations will influence your decision regarding the best time to apply for internship. Other things being equal, the closer you are to the completion of your degree program, the more competitive you will be. Training center staff prefer to help students polish existing clinical skills rather than teach the basics. They also do not want to waste their resources on students who may not complete their academic program. "ABDs" are difficult to place or support, so the further advanced the dissertation, the more favorably an applicant will be regarded.

Preparing to apply for internship

Just as politicians cannot govern until they have been elected, would-be interns cannot begin their training until they have been selected. To get elected, politicians have to conduct a successful campaign; to get accepted at the internship of your choice you will have to go through the application process.

Since it is never too early to begin, I will first describe long term preparations that can be made. If you are reading this book at the last minute, do not despair. These long term preparations are desirable and will make your job easier, but if, like most of us, you tend to put things off until the last minute, you can still prepare an effective application. You will simply have to scurry around a lot more. As Jacob (1987, p. 155) noted, "Gradual preparation would have eased the experience for me. Instead, ignorance and lack of preparation determined that 'internship hunting' was a full-time 2-month job."

Long term preparations. Even if you are not planning to apply for internship for a year or so, there are many things you can do to get ready. One of the most important is what you are doing right now, namely learning about what is involved.

Although a few start in July, most internship years begin on or about September 1. Unless you plan to return to your university after your internship, your strategy should be to complete whatever pre-internship goals you have established, such as collecting your dissertation data, defending your prospectus or having your wedding, before you depart. Once you are on internship you will find you have very little time available for any of these activities. So in the year prior to your departure, arrange your academic and social calendar so that you will have accomplished whatever objectives you have established. Make sure to leave enough time for the actual internship application process.

In anticipation of applying for internship, review the CVs of successful intern applicants from your program. How do your qualifications compare with theirs? Are there things you can do to improve your credentials in the year to come to make your application more competitive? This might be the time to take some specialized clinical courses or sign up for professional workshops in areas such as minority mental health, neuropsychological assessment, geropsychology and other areas of particular interest to internship training facilities. If you have some specialized skills such as a basic knowledge of Spanish or American Sign Language, this might be a good time to polish them up so you can present yourself as having competency in this area. If you have been meaning to write up your master's thesis for presentation or publication, this would be a good time to do so and submit it. In short, while there is time, consider ways you can make your CV stand out as being special when it is compared with those of other applicants.

If you are in a clinical practicum, you can start preparing a work sample for submission along with your application to those internships which require one. Begin by discussing this with your supervisor. You will need to select a subject who will afford you the opportunity to display your clinical skills. Before, you start you will have to obtain informed consent and a release to allow you to use the materials, suitably disguised, in conjunction with your application.

You can also start keeping a detailed log in which you record all your practicum and supervision hours, the names and credentials of your supervisors, the number and the nature of the clients you have seen, the types of treatment in which you have participated, and a record of the various assessment devices you have administered, scored and interpreted. This will be very helpful when you prepare your Curriculum Vitae. (See Chapter Five.)

You can also begin your preliminary reconnaissance, identifying and investigating internships that might interest you. If you start doing this a year in advance, you can benefit from the experiences of the people in the class ahead of you while they are applying for internships. They are going to be very busy and rather tense, so they may not want to spend a lot of time educating you. However, if you offer to help them by writing for brochures or assisting in preparing some of their numerous application forms, you will be more welcome. In particular, if you volunteer to help out by taking them to the airport and later meeting their planes when they return from interviews, you will not only be assisting them but also learning first hand from seasoned veterans. This will be greatly appreciated, since it seems to be an FAA regulation that the only flights intern applicants can take leave before dawn and return after midnight. (If they are scheduled to return at a civilized time, Murphy's Law stipulates that the flight will be delayed.)

Chapter Four recommends attending professional meetings as a cost-effective way to observe and meet personnel from internships that interest you. A number of regional meetings are held in the Spring, the American Psychological Association has its annual meeting in August, and AABT meets in the Fall. AABT typically has an internship forum where students can meet the training directors and learn about a number of programs.

Advance financial planning can also help. Applying for internship can be expensive. Putting aside some funds, taking advantage of sales, and making reservations well in advance may make it less necessary to float a last minute loan.

Short term preparation. While it is never too early to start planning, realistically the bulk of the effort involved in applying for internship will take place   the year you apply. The internship application and selection season begins in the Fall semester and runs through the second Monday in February. I have offered internship application workshops in March and April where not a single student signed up; six months later they are oversubscribed. This chapter will provide a general schedule of what must be done. We will be idealistic and start in the Spring of the year you plan to apply, even though I realize it is unlikely you will actually begin until that Fall.

Your university or professional school probably has certain basic requirements that you must meet before you can submit any applications. These may include passing your comprehensive examinations, completing certain didactic courses, accumulating a specified number of practicum hours, or defending your dissertation prospectus. The Spring semester before you plan to apply, make sure you know what all these requirements are and that you will be able to satisfy them by Fall when you plan to apply. When you have formulated a timetable for meeting these require-ments and other goals you may have established, such as beginning your dissertation or completing certain required or elective courses, meet with your major professor. Discuss your plans and see if your major professor thinks they are realistic.

Once you have secured the general approval of your major professor, meet with your DCT to discuss your plans and get advice. It is also a good idea to meet with your clinical supervisor(s) to determine if they feel you are ready for intern-ship from a clinical standpoint. These three peo-ple, your major professor, your DCT, and your current clinical supervisor, are the individuals you will be asking to write letters of recommenda-tions, so listen to what they have to say. If they have any reservations about your readiness for internship, you want to learn it while you can still do something to remedy the problem. Don't wait until it is time for them to write their letters of recommendation to discover they feel you are deficient in some area. If all goes well, they will approve your plans. (They will also have reason to note how mature, well organized and responsi-ble you are when they write their letters of recommendation.)

Self evaluation. Once you have your timetable approved and made plans to satisfy all your academic goals and requirements, examine your credentials from a Training Director's point of view. As we shall see, different internships have vastly different expectations and requirements. Nevertheless, they are all seeking applicants who can hit the ground running, people who can quickly assume a professional role in, and capably represent, the Psychology Department, albeit as a trainee.

Next year, when you are actually an intern, you may well be asked to help screen applications. Put yourself in this role now, and ask yourself how you would evaluate your own resume. Is this someone you would recommend? Why? If you can get some input from local practitioners or clinical supervisors, so much the better. Articles on the criteria used by internships to rate prospective applicants may also be helpful; several such readings are contained in the chapter on "Selection" in Dana and May's (1987) book Internship training in professional psychology. The purpose of this exercise is to identify possible weaknesses or areas that can be improved while there is still time to do something about it.

One student who went through this exercise one summer decided that he needed more experience in personality assessment with adult inpatients. As DCT, I was able to arrange for him to obtain supervised experience in such a setting during the Fall semester. I also made a point of noting in my letter of recommendation how this student had demonstrated professional maturity and eagerness to learn by taking an unpaid position two afternoons a week to enhance his skills in this area in preparation for internship. Concrete behavior such as this is much more impressive to a Training Director than the banal platitudes usually found in letters of recommendation.

Enhancing your academic credentials. Internships differ in the weight they attach to publications. Some say they are irrelevant, others state they are extremely important. One member of the Selection Committee at an internship housed in a major school of medicine remarked that he flips to the back of the CV and counts the publications before deciding whether to read the rest of the application. I hope he was jesting, but it is a fact that all of our students who have been accepted at that internship have had strong publication records.

Fortunately there are often steps you can take to enhance your CV to make it more competitive. This is a good task for the summer before you apply, but even the Fall of your application year is not too late. If you have been putting off writing up your master's thesis or some other study, now is the time to prepare it for publication and submit it. You can list it as "under review," and even if it is later rejected it will still enhance your CV while it is being evaluated. Similarly take the time to prepare proposals for local or regional professional meetings. If you have collaborated on some research with some faculty members who have been dilatory about getting it written up, fuss at them or offer to write it up yourself.

Admissions committees are also favorably impressed by a commitment to the profession. A time-effective way to enhance your CV is to join professional societies and to enroll in some specialized workshops for continuing education credit. If you belong to a graduate student organization at your university or in your state, the next time the opportunity comes to volunteer to head a committee or to stand for office, go ahead and put yourself forward. This will enable your DCT to comment on the high regard in which your peers hold you and how you have demonstrated leadership. These are little things, to be sure, but they will help differentiate your CV from those of other students who have not engaged in these activities.

Forming a support group. Programs differ greatly in the amount of assistance and support they provide for their internship applicants. As you can see from this book, we do a great deal to prepare our applicants. If you are enrolled in a similar program, do what you are told, even if it conflicts with my advice. It is very important that everyone in a program works together; if you are marching to a different drummer you will have problems.

It is especially important that you meet whatever deadlines your program establishes. Missing a deadline may not seem like a big deal, but it often creates a lot of extra work for the faculty and staff. It can take me longer to process one late letter of recommendation than it does to do the entire batch of letters that were ready on schedule.

If you are in a program that does not provide a great deal of assistance, there is a lot you can do to make the application process easier. I suggest that you form a support group of fellow applicants and work together to make things easier. For example, we provide our students with a copy of the latest APPIC Directory of Internship and Postdoctoral Programs in Professional Psychology which is published annually in July or August. The Directory is essential. It not only describes all the internships, but is also the only source for the address and phone numbers of the various programs. If your school does not do so already, perhaps you can suggest that they subscribe to APPIC. The cost for graduate programs to subscribe is currently $100.00 which includes a copy of the Directory, the APPIC Newsletter, which contains important information about APPIC policies, access to the APPIC Clearinghouse, and a discount on additional copies of the Directory for graduate students in good standing. If your program has subscribed, you can purchase your own copy of the Directory for $15.00, which is half the regular price. Include a letter from your school certifying you are a student in a subscribing program.

If your program prefers not to subscribe, then I suggest that you chip in and order a Directory for your support group. Obtaining the Directory used to be a hassle since APPIC had no permanent address until recently. In the late 1980s, APPIC found the resources to establish a small (130 square feet) Central Office in Washington and hire a full time administrator. Shortly after the first edition of this book was published, they moved to larger quarters. As the second edition of this book goes to press, the current address is:

APPIC Central Office
C/O Ms. Connie Hercey, MPA
733 15th St., NW, Suite 717
Washington, D.C. 20005
Phone: (202) 347-0022
Fax: (202) 393-0079

Ms. Hercey assures me APPIC has a three year lease and should remain at that location for the foreseeable future. If, however, you do not get a response in a reasonable time, it may be they have moved again and you will have to track them down.

Our clinical program also maintains a file of the many brochures that are mailed out annually by internships all across the country. No doubt your program receives them as well. If there is no systematic procedure for making them available, I suggest that you volunteer to undertake the responsibility of creating and maintaining a file for them in some convenient location. One word of advice: get a date stamp and date them as they come in. Otherwise you will soon find current brochures intermingled with those that are hopelessly out of date.

Similarly, a support group can divide up the chores of writing for information, share impressions of internships, and see to it that you do not interfere with one another. Many internships will not take two people from the same program. By coordinating your applications you can cut down on the competition within your group. We have found that mutual cooperation enhances everyone's chances.

Your responsibilities. No matter how supportive your program, the responsibility for selecting the internship that best meets your needs is yours. You must make sure that you have met all the requirements. You must convince the internships' Selection Committees that you are a person they want to have work and study with them for the coming year.

As a psychologist in training, you may have been told you should not be judgmental. When it comes to selecting an internship, forget it. Making judgments is what the selection process is all about. As you prepare your applications and participate in your interviews, do so in the certain knowledge that you will definitely be judged. At the same time, you must judge yourself and the facilities to determine which is best for you.

This requires doing your homework and learning everything you can about each internship. If at all possible, you should visit each site and meet the training staff in person. In every group of internship applicants I have worked with, some students, after interviewing, return having discovered that some of the celebrated luminaries they had admired from afar proved to be arrogant asses and boors, while others who appeared less prestigious on paper were much more impressive in person. Invariably, after interviewing, one or two candidates eliminate their former top choices from consideration in favor of other programs they had formerly ranked considerably lower.

What to do month by month

In this section, I will provide you with a month by month time line of what should be done the year you actually apply for internship. In the chapters that follow, you will find detailed discussions of <u>how</u> to accomplish these various tasks. This is simply a list, without much explanation of what needs to be done.

<u>September</u>. If you began your preparations six months to a year ago, you should be in good shape. If you are like most people who are planning to apply this Fall, you are probably just beginning to think about what needs to be done. Get to work; you have a lot to do:

1. Read this entire book as soon as possible. Don't worry about the details; you will come back to them as you do each step. Just get an overall picture of what has to be done between now and February.

2. If, after skimming the book, you are convinced there is no way you can possibly accomplish everything that must be done in the time you have left given all your other commitments, you may be right. If it looks like you will have serious problems meeting some important goal in the time remaining, it may be better to wait and apply next year.

One year, one of our students who was employed half time and carrying an average course load told me that during the Fall semester she planned to a) complete her major area paper, which in our program is equivalent to the Comprehensive Examination, b) apply for internship, and c) have her wedding and go on her honeymoon. I advised her that this seemed to be an overly ambitious schedule and suggested that she cut it back somewhat. However, she was sure she could do it all; for example, she felt her Caribbean honeymoon would afford her ample opportunity to complete her major area paper and fill out her internship applications. By the time the semester had ended, she had actually managed to maintain her employment and her course load and accomplish two of her three goals. I thought this was a triumph, but she was very disappointed.

(Sorry, but it is none of your business which two she completed.)

3. If you have not done all the things that I suggested you should do last Spring, take care of them now. That is, make sure you will meet all the requirements for going on internship this Fall, meet with your major professor, DCT and clinical supervisors, discuss your plans, get feedback, and work out a schedule to accomplish all the necessary tasks in the time allotted.

4. If you have already prepared a resume or CV, update it and do what you can to enhance it as noted above. If you have never prepared a CV, read Chapter Five and start to work on it. To help you assemble and record the information you will need, go to your local Post Office, ask for "Standard Form 171" and start filling it out.

5. Read Chapter Three and prepare your list of priorities. If you have dependents or are involved in relationships with people who will be affected by your decisions, it is time for some serious conversations. Are you going to go alone, or will one or more people go with you? Either way, their needs will influence your choice of an internship site.

Whether or not other people are involved in your decision, some brainstorming with your support group and discussions with former interns and faculty will also help you in establishing priorities.

6. Start reviewing the APPIC _Directory_. As you identify places in which you are interested, write for brochures. (Some especially well-organized students ask if they should write earlier. It is better to wait. Many internships update their brochures annually, and if you write before September you may get a leftover copy of last year's brochure.)

7. Prepare for travel by joining automobile and airline frequent traveler and hotel discount clubs. Be alert for Fall luggage and clothing sales.

hanging carrier

8. Get a flu shot.

October. In October, I schedule individual meetings with the intern applicants to discuss their priorities and the various sites that they have included on their preliminary lists. They also bring their CVs to this meeting. We go over them in detail, and I make suggestions on how they can be improved. These interviews provide the students with feedback and they give me information that I can use in preparing my letters of recommendation. If your program does not have some comparable procedure, I suggest you seek out your DCT and/or major professor for a similar session.

In any case, whether or not you are going to have such a meeting, by the end of October and preferably before you should have:

1. Completed your list of personal priorities to be used in evaluating internships.

2. Formulated a preliminary list of possible sites and started to evaluate them in the light of your priorities.

3. Completed your CV.

After meeting with your DCT or advisor and revising your list of potential sites, you should:

4. Write each site for application forms if you have not already done so.

5. Go to the Registrar's Office and order transcripts to be sent to each place you are considering.

6. Get that flu shot you have been

putting off.

November. Each internship will have its own individual date by which all materials must be received. However, the earliest due date drives the overall schedule since it is easiest and safest to send everything out at once. In recent years this date has been the last Friday in November. Since university mail rooms and offices are closed over the Thanksgiving holiday, this means you should plan for everything being placed in the mail at the Post Office by noon on Wednesday, the day before Thanksgiving.

To accomplish this:

1. Provide your major professor, DCT, and clinical supervisor with copies of your CV and a list of addresses to which letters are to be sent. Make sure the addresses are complete as noted in Chapter Six, and follow to the letter whatever you are told to do with regard to postage and so on.

2. Complete all your application forms, personal statements, cover letters and CVs and mail them by that Wednesday.

3. Make sure all your letters of recommendation and your transcripts have actually been sent. (I have known major professors who wrote the letters but forgot to mail them.)

4. If you hope to visit internship facilities during Christmas break, you may have to obtain advance purchase tickets during November. Unfortunately, those facilities that interview by invitation only will probably not be ready to decide whom they should invite, so don't be surprised if they put off your request for an appointment. Whether or not you actually need to purchase tickets, given all the holiday travel, the sooner you can book reservations the better, especially if there is no penalty for changes or cancellations. *through travel agent & hold them*

December. By the beginning of the second week in December, all the internships should have received and filed your applications and supporting materials. Call and find out if your application is complete. If not, send in any missing items as soon as possible.

Now is the time to arrange for interviews and make your travel plans. If you have not already done so, start scheduling appointments. Some popular places do not have the time to interview everyone, and latecomers may be out of luck. If you cannot visit in person, arrange for a telephone interview. Before your first internship visit, dress up and do some role playing with faculty members or the other applicants in your support group, using the questions in Appendix Five.

If you have not gotten your flu shot by the end of December, forget it. It is too late to do any good. Budget time for being sick when you return, and stock up on tissues and chicken soup.

January. This is when you will do most of your interviewing. It is also the time when the weather is apt to be poorest for traveling. Follow the advice in Chapters Seven and Eight, and be sure to keep in touch with your home base so you can receive messages from other internships.

After you have returned from interviewing, compare notes with the other internship applicants, seek the advice of faculty and friends, and rank the places to which you have applied. If you have some remaining questions, now is the time to call and ask. If you were unable to do so during your visit, talking with some of the present interns might help. Send thank you notes to the places you visited.

If there are any places you are not willing to attend, consider withdrawing your candidacy. If your list has gotten too short, consider filing some more applications.

Even though Uniform Notification day is not until the second Monday in February, some Training Directors will start calling the last week in January, ostensibly to see if you have any questions but actually to try to ascertain whether you are a viable candidate. Review Chapter Nine and the APPIC rules in Appendix One so you will be prepared to respond.

February. From Ground Hog Day until Notification Day, you can expect to receive calls from Training Directors trying to determine how you rank their programs. Some TDs will not call you, but they will be paying close attention to whether or not you call or write them. If they do not hear from you, they may conclude that you are not interested. If you are seriously interested in an internship, you should definitely touch base with them during this period. *call*

No matter who calls whom, it is absolutely essential that as soon as possible you formulate a ranked list of desirable placements and stick with it. Your response to a call from your first choice will differ from your reply to one that is ranked lower. As noted in the last chapter on the "Endgame," when talking to TDs, be absolutely honest. Tell the truth and nothing but the truth, but do not feel that you have to tell the whole truth.

Your DCT and, possibly, your major professor will probably be receiving similar calls from TDs attempting to ascertain the likelihood various applicants will attend their programs. Keep your DCT informed as to your preferences, and see if he or she will contact the internships you are most interested in to find out how you stand. Consult with your DCT about the advisability of sending a commitment letter to your first choice. If you learn that your first choice is a long shot, you may want to give more encouragement to programs ranked lower.

Notification Day. Your school will probably give you a set of instructions to follow on Notification Day. If so, comply with them exactly. Otherwise, follow the instructions in Chapter Nine.

Formal notification of candidates begins at 9:00 AM, CST, the second Monday in February. When you receive an offer, you must indicate if you accept, reject or will "hold" the offer. If you hold it, you have until 4:00 PM CST to decide whether or not to accept the offer. During that time, the internship cannot retract the offer, nor can they offer that position to anyone else. You can hold only one offer at a time, and if you have not accepted by 4:00 PM CST, the offer is rescinded and the program can offer the slot to someone else.

Once you accept an offer on Notification Day, you have made a binding commitment that you cannot break. The internship marks that slot as being filled and for you the internship selection season is over. You must immediately notify any program whose offer you were holding, and, as a courtesy, you should inform the other sites where you applied that you are no longer available. Then you can go celebrate.

After Notification Day. After Notification Day, when you have accepted an offer from the internship of your choice, send a formal letter of acceptance to the TD with a copy to your DCT. This should include your understanding of all the details of the agreement you have reached.

You should shortly be receiving a confirmation letter from the internship. If you do not receive one within a reasonable period of time, you or your DCT should check with the program to make sure there is no problem.

It is also appropriate to send nice notes to those places that made you offers which you did not choose to accept. Remember, soon after you

51

complete your internship you will be out there again looking for a job.

CHAPTER THREE:

ESTABLISHING YOUR PRIORITIES

The first step in applying for an internship is probably the most important. This is establishing your priorities: deciding what it is you are looking for in your internship. If you do this honestly and insightfully at the outset, all the remaining steps will be infinitely easier. On the other hand if you put this step off or fail to discern your real needs, the whole application process will be much more difficult, especially the final stages in which you must come to some definite decisions.

I cannot overemphasize the importance of analyzing your priorities in the very beginning, before you start surveying the Directory, writing for brochures, composing your resume, and preparing your applications. Each person's needs and goals are different; there is no one internship that is best for everyone. Take the time to reflect on what it is you want from your internship.

You may find it helpful to formalize this process by listing all the features you do and do not want in an internship setting. Weigh the importance of each by indicating whether you regard it as "essential," "important," or "desirable." Use this list to "score" possible places. After you have refined this checklist and gathered more information, you can use it to help you decide which programs you will apply to, and, later, to help you rank your choices. It is because every person's list is unique that there is no internship that is ideal for everyone.

There are two sets of factors to consider in evaluating internships, professional and personal. The first set has to do with the training you will

your criteria of interest (handwritten margin note)

receive. These include whether a program has APA approval, the nature of the setting, the population(s) you will be exposed to, the rotations available, and the personnel with whom you would be working. The second set has to do with quality of life. It includes such aspects as geography, family ties and finances. I will discuss a few of the most common considerations below.

Professional considerations

There are many factors to consider in evaluating an internship program. Important considerations are whether or not a program is approved by the American Psychological Association and whether the internship is for one year or two. With regard to the nature of the training offered, you need to consider whether you prefer diversity or wish to specialize, if the number or the nature of the rotations available is important to you, and how you value the opportunity to attend didactic presentations and seminars. The training faculty is extremely important. Their expertise, theoretical orientation, accessibility and commitment to training are all factors you must weigh. The facilities and equipment that are provided and the opportunity to do research will be more critical for some applicants than others; you will have to decide for yourself how you weight these aspects. Less tangible, but still influential, is the atmosphere that prevails; this includes morale, collegiality and the degree of respect or rivalry that may prevail among different services or disciplines. The prestige of an institution, and the degree to which it fits with your perception of your present training needs and your future plans also need to be considered.

In the pages that follow, I will comment on some of these factors. While I will offer my recommendations and opinions on these issues, this is done with the intent of helping you determine your own attitudes so you can decide which aspects are most important for you. For example, since I value internships for the clinical training they provide, I do not weight opportunities for research very high, but for you this might be a vital consideration. If my comments help you diagnose your feelings, they will accomplish their purpose; on the other hand, if you copy them down and say to yourself that certain things are important because Megargee says they are, you will be missing the point.

After you have formulated your personal list of priorities, when you start evaluating actual programs, you will soon discover that no place will have everything exactly as you would like it. If it fits your professional goals, it may conflict with your personal needs. Inevitably there will be tradeoffs and compromises. You will have to decide for yourself which aspects are most important for you. By establishing your professional priorities at the outset, before they are intertwined with any specific programs, you will be better able to analyze objectively how important these considerations are for you.

APA accreditation. Training programs in professional psychology are accredited by the American Psychological Association. Each year the accreditation status of predoctoral internship training programs is listed in the December issue of the American Psychologist. The APPIC Directory also notes the APA accreditation status as of June 15, when the Directory goes to press. The Directory notes the APA accreditation status of each program as being "Full," "Provisional," "Probation," or "None."

The APA Committee on Accreditation (1991, p. 1309) explains, "There are three categories of accreditation. Full accreditation is granted to any program that, in the professional judgment of the Committee, meets the criteria in a satisfactory manner. Provisional accreditation is granted to programs making an initial application that, in the professional judgment of the Committee, do not meet all of the criteria, but for which the Committee believes there is a reasonable expectation that they will be met within a foreseeable period of time from the date of the initial site visit. Probation is the category into which a fully accredited program is placed when the Committee has evidence that it is not currently in satisfactory compliance with the criteria." "None" may mean that the program has not applied for accreditation or that it applied and was not deemed adequate for provisional accreditation.

You should apply only to fully accredited internships, unless there are compelling reasons to attend a program that is not fully approved. Perhaps your personal situation dictates you must stay in a locale which only has a provisionally approved training center; perhaps child care responsibilities require that you take a half-time internship and there are no accredited ones available. As long as you graduate with a doctoral degree from an APA-approved training program, it is usually possible to be licensed even if your internship is not APA-accredited. It is up to your graduate school to determine whether you have satisfied your degree program's predoctoral internship requirement.

So why is it recommended that you should limit yourself to APA-accredited internships? First, even though it is usually possible to obtain a license or other credentials, such as a listing in the National Register of Health Service Providers in Psychology, this could change. Future legislation might be more stringent. The primary reason, however, is the hassle involved. The typical license application asks if you completed a one year APA-accredited predoctoral internship. If you did, you simply check "Yes" and go on to the next part of the application. If you check "No," however, you will probably need to describe and document all the details of your internship experience so the authorities can judge whether it was equivalent to a an APA-accredited program. This may include the number and the nature of the clients you saw, the various rotations on which you served, the number of hours of supervision you received, and, if that was not enough, you may have to establish all your supervisors' qualifications and credentials. The older you get, the more difficult this becomes. It is far better to apply only to programs with full accreditation.

One year or two year internship. To graduate with a degree in clinical psychology from an APA approved doctoral program, you must have a one year predoctoral internship. Most states, however, require an additional year of supervised postdoctoral experience before you can be licensed. In 1987, a National Conference on Internship Training in Psychology was held in Gainesville, FL, at which it was recommended that a two-year internship, one year predoctoral and one year postdoctoral, be required (Belar, Bieliauskas, Larsen, Mensh, Poey, & Roehlke, 1987). Blom (1990, p. 7) recently noted, "Should prescription privileges become a reality...the additional training required may add further weight to the arguments that two years of internship are not only desirable but necessary to ensure adequate preparation for the practice of professional psychology." Moreover, there is also general agreement that specialty training in areas such as pediatric psychology, neuropsychological assessment, and forensic psychology will typically require one or more years of additional postdoctoral education. As a result of all these considerations, some internships now stipulate that they are for two years.

It is up to you to decide whether to apply for a one or two year internship. If you have had relatively little practicum experience, or if you are seeking specialty training, a two-year internship makes more sense than if you have already had considerable experience and have more general interests. I do not foresee APA requiring two years. Even if it did, it would not be retroactive.

Diversity vs. specialization. Some programs such as those in pediatric psychology provide very focused and specialized training. Others require a variety of more general experiences. Which is best for you?

Other things being equal, I suggest you seek diversity. Your predoctoral internship may be the last chance for you to get such a varied experience. The broader the range of clinical cases, approaches, and settings, the better.

I also recommend that you choose a setting that will complement your previous practicum experience. If all your work has been with outpatients, now is the time to get some inpatient experience. If you have been working at a prison, consider a medical setting and so on.

Look beyond the specific facility and determine what other opportunities exist in the area. Often there will be a number of hospitals or agencies that are geographically contiguous and one can attend colloquia or Grand Rounds at neighboring facilities, or even have a rotation there. Visiting one VA hospital, I discovered it was across the street from a major children's hospital so that it was possible for the VA interns to do a pediatric rotation even though it was not mentioned in the brochure.

Number of rotations available. While I favor diversity, do not be seduced by the sheer number of rotations that are listed for some internships. An internship is not like a buffet or salad bar where you can have a little bit of everything. Instead it is like ordering a fixed price family dinner in a Chinese restaurant: you get one choice from Column A, two from Column B and so on. Moreover, just as everyone automatically gets rice and a fortune cookie, you will probably be required to take certain rotations. For example, it is common to require all interns to have be involved in both assessment and treatment, to work with both children and adults, and to have both inpatient and outpatient rotations over the course of a year.

There is only a finite amount you can experience within a year. You will probably have two, possibly three, major rotations and two or three minor ones. However, you may simply be assigned to one setting for six months and another for the remaining six months, especially in a consortium in which the various participating institutions are miles apart from one another. In such internships, it is up to the interns and their supervisors to work out a varied array of experiences within each facility.

You will usually be expected to pick up three or four long term therapy cases in your first rotation and carry them throughout the year. In addition, there will usually be a standard array of seminars for everyone plus some electives. Given all these obligations, your degrees of freedom are limited.

A vital consideration is who gets to participate in the various rotations. Some internships' brochures display an extraordinary number of rotations. Closer examination may reveal that several are funded from particular sources such as a specialized hospital within a consortium or a foundation focused on a specific disorder. If so, the interns who receive those stipends may spend a major portion of their time in those settings and have relatively little opportunity to learn about the other settings except over coffee with fellow interns. Moreover, it may be that only the interns on those stipends get to work in those areas, especially if highly specialized skills such as administering a neuropsychological assessment battery are required.

Many settings have track-specific selection in which applicants are chosen for particular rotations. Such commitments are part of the bargaining process prior to Notification Day. If it is especially important to you to have a specific rotation or to work with a particular faculty member, you need to find out how these assignments are made and determine whether you are likely to obtain this position. It does you no good to have an item on the menu if you can't order it.

In short, before you pass over an internship that has a relatively small selection of rotations in favor of one with a wider variety, determine how much of the variety you will actually be able to experience. It may be that you will discover that in both settings you would have pretty much the same program.

Didactic training and seminars. Some internships offer a wealth of didactic training and seminars with top-notch people in their fields. In contrast to the university courses you are familiar with, these are more apt to be mini-seminars with one to three sessions devoted to a given clinical topic or proseminars with a series of experts discussing their specialties. Grand Rounds and case conferences are another important aspect of internship training.

Since internships vary greatly in their resources and their geography, the opportunities to participate in these additional educational experiences will differ. You must decide for yourself how much weight you will place on this aspect of internship training.

Personnel. More important than the specific rotations, the populations available, and all the other aspects of the curriculum, are the actual people with whom you will be working. These include the Director of Training, your supervisors, and the other interns.

Good Training Directors are sincerely interested in their students and the quality of their educational experience. If necessary, they are ready to do battle with the administration to preserve the quality of the interns' education and prevent them from being exploited. Poor ones are hassled, disinterested and looking for ways out. If their morale is low, yours will probably suffer as well.

How do you discriminate the good from the poor? Tenure in office is no reliable criterion; some who have been directors for many years continue because of their commitment to training, but there are other long term directors who are obviously burned out and waiting for retirement. A new director may be excited and filled with ideas to improve training or resentful over the time that is required. I am always interested in whether the TD sought out the post or was stuck with it because no one else wanted it. In any event, ask the present interns about the dedication, enthusiasm and accessibility of the TD.

Supervisors are also very important. Most of your actual training will take place in one-to-one interactions with individual supervisors. More than any other single factor, a good supervisor can make a rotation, while a poor one can be devastating. You may have to dig a bit to learn about the nature, quality and quantity of supervision, but it will be one of the single most important aspects of your training.

In evaluating a facility, you may be dazzled by the eminent names listed on the brochure and the chance to work with such people. That is fine, but make sure you establish whether these individuals actually supervise trainees, whether they will be available the year you intern, and whether you have any say over who you get as a supervisor.

Supervisors are not always people on staff. When I was at the Palo Alto VA on a practicum, I was assigned a chronic schizophrenic who had been hospitalized for 14 years as my long-term individual psychotherapy case. Not a likely prospect. However, I also had an outside consultant from Stanford named Albert Bandura as a supervisor who made it an excellent learning experience.

The other interns will be your primary support group during your training. They may become your best friends or your worst enemies. While each class is somewhat different, observing the present interns and their interactions can give you some clues about the types of people selected, and whether the institutional atmosphere is divisive or congenial. Are they all Type A's, or more laid back? Are they doctrinaire and rigid, or tolerant of differing opinions? Are they trustworthy or treacherous?

Sometimes you can pick up important clues when you are given a tour of the interns' offices. I recently visited an internship in which three trainees shared an office they had decorated with numerous snapshots of the three of them and their families socializing together on Halloween, Thanksgiving and other occasions. A series of charts on the wall, to which they had all contributed, recorded the amusing things their child clients had said, and done, to them during the course of the rotation. Clearly this was a congenial group.

Theoretical orientations. Settings differ greatly in theoretical orientation. Some places are very formal and authoritarian, expecting everyone to formulate and discuss cases according to the "official" orientation, whether it be behavioral or dynamic. Other places are more flexible and enjoy a wide range of viewpoints among the students and staff.

Your own theoretical orientation and your degree of commitment to it will be of interest to the internships, as theirs will be to you. While a setting will probably not require that you share their frame of reference, they will expect you to be open to exploring their point of view. Moreover, you should have a sufficient grasp of the basic principles and vocabulary of the prevailing orientation so as to be able to understand what is being said.

Other things being equal, you will probably learn more from a setting with a variety of viewpoints than one with a single party line. One intern I visited had six different supervisors with as many orientations. She learned to shift smoothly from a psychoanalytic to an ego psychology to a cognitive behavioral to a radical behavioral frame of reference in the course of an afternoon as she went from one supervisor to the next.

This intern's experience brings up another issue with regard to supervisors. Where are they located? In the case of this intern, they were consultants on soft money who were located in their practices around town and it was necessary for her to travel to them. In other settings, most supervision will occur on the premises, even if the supervisors are not on staff. Not only does this mean they will be more readily available for consults, but also that they are more likely to attend case conferences.

Service vs. training. Internships vary in their commitment to training. This is reflected in the number of hours allotted for supervision, in the number of seminars offered, and in the number of cases you are expected to process. Are you expected to give minimal batteries and turn out as many reports as possible, or are you encouraged to try various techniques and given an opportunity to read and reflect on a puzzling case? In some programs, the interns feel they are being exploited and used to provide low-cost service to the facility with minimal educational benefits. In others, interns are expected to "eat what they kill" by generating fees that will compensate the agency for their stipends and supervision.

This is best established by discussions with present interns during your site visit. You can also raise this issue with the training staff as long as you make it clear you are concerned about the quality of the training and not the quantity of work.

Facilities and equipment. The facilities that are available can also influence the quality of the supervision and training. Some internships have superb equipment, others do not. I recently toured one setting in which each intern had an office in which he or she could see clients. Each office was equipped with a complete video recording setup...camera, VCR and monitor... for taping sessions. Supervisors' offices were similarly equipped. Another internship had two cameras in every therapy room feeding to a central control console worthy of MGM Studios. There, technicians could alternate cameras to catch questions and responses in a dyadic therapy session in one room, while maneuvering the play room camera angles by remote control to track children as they scurried about. When I read the evaluations of the students interning at these settings, it was obvious that the supervisors could and did closely monitor the actual therapy process and provided the trainees with detailed feedback.

Few places have such superb equipment. However, the availability of audio and video recording equipment, computers, electronic test scoring apparatus, and specialized equipment for neuropsychological assessment, biofeedback and the like obviously has an impact on what can be done there. *technicians for testing etc.?*

Opportunities for research. For some students the opportunity to do dissertation research is important. If you have to do a great deal of dissertation work on internship, perhaps you ought to consider waiting another year and applying after you have completed your dissertation. Having a well advanced or completed dissertation will not only give you an edge on other applicants, but will also make it easier to move smoothly from your internship into a full time professional or academic position. More and more Training Directors are maintaining that a completed dissertation, or at least a defended prospectus, should be required before students apply for internship.

You may be told there is ample time available for you to do your research even when there is not. Except for a few places that are very academically oriented, do not count on having much time for personal research. If you are the sort of person who took a big pile of "important" books home to read over Christmas or summer vacations <u>and</u> <u>actually</u> <u>read</u> <u>them</u>, maybe you will be able to accomplish a fair amount on internship, but most interns find there is so much clinical work to do that they quickly lose their academic mind set. After spending 60 to 70 hours seeing clients, attending staffings, writing reports, receiving supervision and participating in seminars, you will probably have little inclination for crunching numbers or writing technical prose. I personally feel that spending a lot of time on your dissertation can detract from what should be a unique clinical experience. Your major professor will probably disagree.

A few academically oriented internships do offer rich opportunities to collaborate with faculty in their ongoing research projects. This may enable you to get shared authorship on several publications. However, even in these settings it is unlikely you will be able to formulate and carry out a personal research project. Given the amount of time it takes to settle in, observe the opportunities available, write a proposal, and get it approved, it is difficult to do much data collection in the span of a one-year internship, especially since you will be rotating through a variety of settings. If you plan to stay for two years, however, research can often occupy a larger portion of your available time in the second year.

<u>Relations</u> <u>with</u> <u>other</u> <u>disciplines</u>. The professional relations among disciplines should also be considered. They may be reflected in the formal table of organization which indicates who reports to whom; i.e. does the Chief of Psychology report to the Chief of Psychiatry? However, it is the personal relationships and mutual respect between professionals from different disciplines that are most important.

The tensions between psychology and psychiatry on the national scene can be reflected in the relations between these disciplines in some medical settings. If the psychology interns wear white coats and are called "residents," I usually infer that psychology has a status problem vis a vis psychiatry.

As a psychology intern you may get caught up in these factional disputes. One of my students was reprimanded by a psychiatric resident because he had the temerity to write a "diagnostic impression" ("patient appears depressed") in a chart, thus usurping the exclusive right of physicians to make medical diagnoses. The resident complained to the Chief of Psychiatry who complained to the Chief of Psychology. Eventually, a formal hearing was held before it all got worked out. Presumably all of this occurred because everyone wanted to make sure that the patient received the best possible care, but somehow I never learned how the client benefited from all this wrangling. You may enjoy such confrontations, but from my standpoint, with everything else you have to worry about on internship who needs this sort of bovine residue?

Politics and purges. Apart from interdisciplinary harmony, as you travel around the circuit you may hear rumors about high level political struggles in which administrators resign or are fired. Sometimes these struggles are real, sometimes simply gossip. They are usually conveyed in hushed tones by some interns who are presently at the facility and are eager to display their inside knowledge of programmatic politics. The implication is that you should avoid that setting until the conflicts have been resolved or new people appointed.

An unstable political climate, if in fact it exists, is certainly a factor to consider, but its effects should not be overemphasized. To put the matter in perspective, suppose that as a graduate student you teach introductory psychology to undergraduates at your university. If the Chancellor of the University System fired the President of your school, would it really make any difference in the quality of instruction for the freshmen enrolled in your class? At the intern level, these political battles, unlike the territorial disputes described above, probably have relatively little impact.

Prestige. Some internships are more prestigious than others. Graduating from an eminent internship enhances your vita and may open some doors. It also makes your DCT look good. However, prestige does not necessarily guarantee that the training afforded interns is better, or even as good, as it may be at other, less renowned facilities. The famous people whose names add luster to a program's reputation may spend most of their time off doing the things that make them famous instead of working with the trainees. It is up to you how important an institution's prestige is to you and weigh it accordingly.

Fit with your training needs. In reviewing your readiness for internship, you will no doubt conclude that you are well prepared in certain areas and adequate in several others, but that there are some professional skills that need to be enhanced. Unless you plan to be a Renaissance psychologist, it is unlikely that you want to achieve the highest levels of proficiency in all areas. I am pretty good at using traditional assessment techniques, but I doubt if I ever will have occasion to measure evoked potentials.

In formulating your priorities for internship, you need to establish some training goals. What is it you want to accomplish during your internship year? Consult with your faculty advisors and clinical supervisors. What are the areas you most need to work on? With what patient populations and treatment settings should you gain more experience? By asking yourself and your mentors these questions, you should be able to formulate a list of the types of training experiences and rotations you are going to seek on internship, as well as an idea of how much you want to emphasize various areas.

Fit with future plans. Every applicant has different career goals. Consider what you want to be doing five and ten years from now. When evaluating possible programs, keep these objectives in mind and ask yourself how each setting will influence your chances of achieving your ambitions. If, for example, you plan on postdoctoral training in a particular area, will this internship prepare you for the postdoctoral program and enhance your chances of getting accepted?

Look beyond the professed goals of the training program and examine the actual achievements of its graduates. What kinds of jobs do they get? What are they doing five years later? Some places that profess to prepare you for academic positions, for example, may have virtually all of their former interns enter professional practice.

importance of intern placement

Some Training Directors and their staffs work very hard at helping their interns find full time positions at the conclusion of their internship. Obviously this is easiest when the student has completed the dissertation and the facility is located in the area where the student hopes to locate. Other internships do not regard intern placement as part of their responsibility and do not get involved with this aspect. Such assistance will be more important to some students than to others.

The importance of how well the program fits with your future plans is clearly evident if you consider interning in one of the military programs. Military internships have obvious advantages in terms of initial salary, medical and retirement benefits, and opportunities for foreign travel. However, they require you to spend three years on active duty after completing your internship, even if you have not completed your dissertation. The impact of a military internship on your future career plans is obvious. You need to realize that, even though it is subtler, any internship you choose will also have far-reaching effects on your career. Thus, you should apply the same criterion of fit with future plans to all the settings you consider, military and civilian alike.

Balancing professional priorities. As we have reviewed some of these professional considerations, it may have seemed that some choices were obvious or trivial. Everyone wants high quality training, dedicated supervisors, congenial colleagues and a free choice of desirable rotations. What you must do is decide on their relative importance to you, because you will find that tradeoffs are inevitable. In order to get that neuropsych rotation you covet, you may have to go to a place where there is considerable interdisciplinary strife. An institution with considerable prestige may emphasize service at the expense of training. If you can decide on the relative importance of these professional issues before they get linked to particular places, you will find it easier to evaluate actual internships.

Personal and practical considerations.

In addition to these professional factors, there are personal preferences and practical concerns to consider. Since you are going to spend at least a year of your life in your internship, it is important that you consider these aspects as well as your professional priorities.

Family and personal relationships. Family ties and relationships often play a vital role in selecting a site. Aged or infirm parents may want you to locate near them. If you have a spouse, partner or children, the first big decision that must be made is whether they are going to travel with you to the internship.

Sometimes it is undesirable, impractical or just plain impossible for your loved one(s) to relocate. If this is the case, you may decide to intern close to home. This is obviously much easier in some parts of the country than in others. If your region is rich in training resources, interning near your home base may not present much of a problem. If good local training facilities are scarce, however, the decision to stay near home may mean sacrificing some professional goals such as attending a fully accredited training program.

If you decide to leave your family or friends behind while you go away on internship for a year, accessibility will probably be an important consideration. An internship within driving distance will allow you to come home some weekends. If you must go farther afield, choosing an internship located in a "hub" city will make air travel easier and less expensive.

If family members or partners are going to move with you to the internship site, then their needs for employment, education and so forth will have to be considered along with your training requirements. Having a partner who is unable to find work in a new city can be devastating to a relationship that may already be strained by the stresses induced by the training program.

If you are traveling in tandem with another intern applicant, compromises will be necessary. Some internships make an effort to keep couples together, even when it involves different disciplines such as psychology and social work. Others prefer not to take two people from the same university. This is the sort of issue that can be investigated during the reconnaissance phase.

The best strategy for couples who wish to remain in proximity is for them to limit their applications to a single area. Other things being equal, metropolitan areas with a variety of settings such as Boston, the New York Metropolitan area, the District of Columbia and its environs, Chicago, Houston, Los Angeles, and the San Francisco Bay Area afford couples the best chance to stay together, and it is easier to travel from one major city to another in the Northeast than in the Northwest. If pre-allocated slots are available in your program, it can simplify the problem of couples by getting at least one person pinned down early.

Caring for children is difficult while on internship, especially in those settings that expect 60 to 70 hour work weeks. Some interns rely on their non-interning spouse or other family members to care for their children during the internship year, especially when circumstances dictate it is best to leave the children behind. Others may have to rely on relatives to provide day care; if so, they need to select a program located where they have family members who are willing and able to assist them.

Parents lacking family or other child care resources, may seek other alternatives. Commercial day care for preschool is one possibility, but internship stipends are limited and most communities do not provide adequate public care, especially for new arrivals. Nor do many training programs provide on-site centers. The solution that is most often discussed is the half-time two-year internship that enables parents to complete the APA requirement within 24 months (Blom, 1990, 1991; Ochroch, 1990). Zimet (1991) reports that of the 2,196 APPIC predoctoral internships available in 1991, only 123 (5.6%) are part time, and of these only 45 are APA accredited. Clearly, more such positions would be a great help to parents, although Blom (1991, p.3) recently noted, "Political issues also enter the process; for instance, should half-time internships be available to all applicants regardless of parenting status or gender, or should they be exclusively or preferentially provided only for parents of young children or females with young children? Will this open the door for litigation for discriminatory practices?"

Location. In addition to proximity to family

members, geography is an important consideration for other reasons. You will make many contacts on internship and no doubt generate some job offers. For this reason, it is sensible to consider a site in the area where you eventually plan to locate. Going to Boston will not help you find a job in Southern California.

If you still have your dissertation work to complete, proximity to your university or professional school may be another geographic consideration. If there is a lot of work remaining on your dissertation, you may have to select a site nearby, choose a topic that can be investigated at your new location, or decide to postpone applying for internship.

Geography also interacts with financial concerns. Living expenses are much higher in some places than others. During the application process, you can reduce travel expenses by developing a list of several places in a particular region instead of applying to internships that are scattered all over the continent.

Of course, geographic considerations need not always be practical. If you would like to spend a year in Hawaii or there is some other place you have always wanted to visit, put that down and give it an appropriate weight. Quality of life, rural vs. urban environment, climate, proximity to a beach and similar factors are also worth considering.

Financial considerations. Finances are another factor. Some programs offer unfunded positions. Students whose financial resources permit it sometimes choose an unfunded internship at the setting of their choice rather than settle for a funded position at a less preferred site. I have never favored this strategy. Funded or unfunded, the internship will expect the same workload; I feel that unpaid interns who are working the same hours as the other trainees sooner or later will begin feeling exploited. Of course in certain situations, this may be the only way to get the experience you wish. For example, various regulations limit the stipends available for students who are not U.S. citizens.

Among the funded positions, stipends vary greatly. A survey of our brochures and a recent APPIC Directory (APPIC, 1991a) showed a range from $6,000 to $32,500. Most seem to be in the range from $11,000 to $13,000. Fringe benefits also differ greatly. The setting with the lowest salary offered no fringe benefits, whereas the one with the highest stipend had generous benefits including health care for the trainee and his or her family, housing and subsistence allowances, commissary privileges and paid attendance at workshops and professional meetings.

Pay particular attention to whether medical benefits are provided, especially if you have a family and/or health problems. While you are at it, check and see if your university provides health benefits to interns who are not in residence, and if so, what fees you must pay to keep your health plan active. You may discover that the cost of health insurance makes an enormous difference in the actual value of a stipend.

To people accustomed to the usual graduate school deprivation schedule, a stipend of $11,000 to $13,000 may seem quite adequate. However, you may find that your expenses are significantly higher on internship. Additions to and maintenance of your wardrobe, carfare, and rent will often be higher. You may have to budget travel back to your university, and, if you are separated from a loved one, you can count on the phone bill being higher.

If your graduate school is in a relatively rural region and your internship is in a metropolitan area, you can expect the cost of living, especially rents, to be substantially higher. If your stipend is modest, you may have to live at some distance from the site where housing is more nearly affordable; this increases the time and money spent commuting and decreases the time spent at the facility. Other places may require you to travel back and forth from one facility to another which has the same effect. No one is going to get rich on internship, but if the stipend is so low and/or the living expenses so high that you must take a second job to survive, you will get less out of the experience.

Evaluate the local cost of living by asking other interns and by checking the rents in the classified ads when you visit. If possible, inspect the areas with the rents you will be able to afford on your stipend. Is the neighborhood so bad that you will have to budget $100 a month for ammunition and emergency room expenses? You can ask your insurance agent for the auto liability and theft rates and provisions at possible sites. In addition to their impact on your budget, the rates might be a good unobtrusive index of the relative safety of various locales.

I recently visited one of our interns in the Northeast. He was unable to meet me because his car had been stolen from his driveway. What surprised him most was that when he told the staff at the training center he could not find anyone who had not had a car stolen, or at least boosted. Needless to say, no one had informed him of this probability when he had interviewed at the internship.

You might also want to check your coverage; the intern's car was recovered in another city, but by the time the police notified him, the daily storage charges had accumulated to the point where they exceeded the value of his automobile. The insurance company refused to reimburse him and he was forced to abandon his car.

hours required **Quality of life.** One aspect of an internship that is not readily apparent from the brochures is the pace and the amount of stress placed on interns. Some are frenetic...the interns all carry _beepers?_

beepers and rarely complete a meal or a trip to the bathroom without being summoned to a phone; others are leisurely and laid back. Some places require interns to work 60 hours or more six or seven days a week to keep abreast of their duties; others expect no more than the standard 40 hour, five day work week. What you choose is up to you, but a Type B personality can be miserable in a Type A setting and vice versa.

How rotations are assigned is another important factor influencing intern morale. If the trainees feel that assignments are distributed honestly and fairly, morale is generally good, but any perceived favoritism is corrosive. The worst morale I ever observed was at a program where the trainees had been called in the first Saturday, placed in a room together, given a list of the rotations that had to be covered each quarter, and told to decide among themselves how they were to be distributed. Hours later, the most powerful individuals emerged with all their preferred placements; the rest got what was left as well as a bitter attitude that poisoned the rest of the year for all concerned.

Another potential stressor is the type of clients you will be treating. Psychopaths and sex offenders pose special problems, and a pediatric AIDs or oncology ward requires extraordinary emotional stamina. You need to evaluate yourself on these dimensions and select accordingly, especially if you are applying for specialized programs such as the V.A.'s gerontology slots.

Amenities will vary greatly from one site to the next. I have visited interns ensconced in brand new, beautifully furnished private offices that I would kill for and others that had to share a battered desk in a room crowded with other trainees. Some sites have magnificent, well maintained grounds with ocean views, tennis courts or golf courses; others are in inner city ghettos where staff venture outside only in groups. Availability of secretarial help, the adequacy of the library, the accessibility of parking, and even the quality of the cafeteria can all influence morale.

Negative items

In addition to all the things you are seeking from your internship, there are undoubtedly some other things you do not want. Some of these may simply be things you would prefer not to have to experience. Jacob (1987), for example, did not want an inpatient psychiatry rotation and negatively weighed those internships that had such a requirement. The more inpatient psychiatric time that was required, the more it detracted from the overall score on her "decision grid." Other trainees may want to avoid any settings where they may encounter snow or ice.

You may feel so strongly about some things that they constitute "veto items." This would cause you not to go to a program under any circumstances, no matter how desirable it was in other respects. These items may be professional or personal, rational or irrational. Many students will not consider an internship that does not offer a particular rotation or experience they consider essential. Some may rule out settings with a strong theoretical orientation that is alien to their own. On the personal side, a setting that does not offer health benefits or which does not have adequate job opportunities for a spouse or partner may be considered out of the question.

Whatever these veto items are, you should note them down and make them explicit. By eliminating any settings which have this negative characteristic, you will save yourself a good deal of time. Of course, if you have so many veto items on your list that you are left with only a handful of potential internships, perhaps you should reconsider and be more flexible.

All of these considerations, professional and personal, positive and negative, are unique to each individual. This is why there is no one internship that is best for everyone. It is this that makes internship selection especially difficult for couples. Once you have formulated your list and weighted the various aspects in the abstract, you should then use it to evaluate the various possible programs and decide on which you wish to investigate further. These lists will also guide you to the information you need to gather about each setting.

NOTES

CHAPTER FOUR:

COMPILING YOUR APPLICATION LIST

Once you have established your personal priorities, you need to compile a list of possible internships that you are interested in investigating in greater depth. This is done through the "preliminary reconnaissance." Although students spend hours poring over internship materials, this is probably the easiest part of the process. You already know how to do library research, and, since you have established your priorities, you know what it is you are looking for.

Early explorations

Some preliminary investigation can take place early in your academic career. Everyone has some thoughts about programs that seem attractive for various reasons. Perhaps you have heard about them from faculty or students who interned there. Maybe they are in a part of the country that has always appealed to you. If it is convenient, you might find it helpful to make a preliminary informal visit to the internship site just to get a feel for the place and see what it looks like. If it is a real "turn off," you will save yourself the trouble of applying. However, keep a low profile; most Training Directors have more than enough to do without feeling obliged to entertain casual visitors who may someday apply for internship.

If members of your faculty interned at one of these sites, or if fellow graduate students are presently enrolled there, solicit their opinions. Often current interns return during the course of the year for committee meetings and other academic chores. Ask their major professors when they are likely to be in town, and see if you can schedule some time with them. If they are located at an internship that is not too far away, you might be able to arrange for an informal visit. Failing this, you may write a letter or phone them at home.

Another cost-effective way of reconnoitering is to identify personnel connected with the training sites in which you are interested and observe or make contact with them at regional or national professional meetings such as APA or AABT. If you are really interested, you might write or call in advance to see if they are free for coffee or a chat. Otherwise, attend one of their presentations and introduce yourself afterwards. This will not only give you a chance to study the person during the presentation, but may also be advantageous later if you apply. When you interview, you won't be just another nameless applicant but someone the interviewer has previously met at a professional meeting.

However, unless you are one of those super-organized people who always mail all their Christmas Cards the day after Thanksgiving, you are probably reading this in the Fall of the year you plan to apply and you have not taken any of the above steps. Given the fact you will soon have to begin filling out applications, how do you develop a list of places and check them out?

Using the directories

First you need to survey the lists of available internship facilities. The Directory of Internship Programs in Professional Psychology published annually by APPIC is by far your best source of information. Consult this source first. (If your program does not provide a copy, see Chapter Two for instructions on how to obtain one.)

You will find the APPIC Directory includes a wealth of valuable information on each facility. It lists the names, degrees and Diplomate status of the Chief Psychologist and Training Director, the number of full and part time doctoral level psychologists employed. It provides the training program's complete mailing address and phone number, as well the date applications are due. It indicates the number of full and part time funded and unfunded internship slots expected and, importantly, whether any are reserved for students at a particular school. It stipulates what requirements applicants must meet with regard to citizenship, number of practicum hours completed, progress toward degree and nature of the training programs from which they welcome applications. It states what major and minor rotations are available, the stipend level and fringe benefits afforded and, finally, how many completed applications they received the previous year. This last item, in conjunction with the number of stipends available, is very helpful in determining how competitive a program is. Much of this information is not available in any other source including the internships' brochures.

While the APPIC Directory also includes each program's APA accreditation status, this information could be somewhat dated. The Directory goes to press in June and, of course, the programs provided their data earlier in the year. Moreover, some programs do not update their entries annually. Hence the accreditation status could have changed in the interim. Fortunately, the December issue of the American Psychologist always provides the most recent list of APA-accredited programs; use this source to check the program's current status, especially if the APPIC Directory or the facility's brochure listed the accreditation status as "provisional" or "pending."

Although the APPIC Directory is the best source of information regarding psychology internships, it thus far does not have an index that will guide you to programs with certain specific characteristics. Instead it is organized geographically, first by states and then by cities within states. So, if you do not already have some places in mind, you need to wade through it state by state

and city by city. A support group can make the
task of searching through the Directory easier. If
you are interested in identifying those programs
which have certain attributes, such as a major
child rotation, you can each take a region and
flag the settings with the desired characteristics.

Since the cities are listed in alphabetical
order, tracking down a particular program can be
difficult, especially when it is a consortium involving facilities in several different towns. Although
it may be located in a metropolitan area and have
several urban sites, the actual headquarters may
be in suburb or a smaller town whose name is
unfamiliar.

If geography is not your strong suit, it
helps to keep an atlas handy. I have had students
who wanted to intern in the Los Angeles area who
skipped right over listings for programs in Culver
City, Downey, Irvine, Long Beach, Orange and
Santa Monica, CA. Remember that training programs situated in different states can be geographically contiguous even though their listings
may be at opposite ends of the alphabetically-
ordered Directory; Baltimore, MD is next door to
Washington, DC, and Newark, NJ is just across
the Hudson River from New York, NY. Although it
is not 100% effective, it often helps to check out
programs in communities with the same telephone
area code as the city you are focusing on.

Other sources of data

You may benefit from lists compiled by
professional organizations or journals that reflect
your particular interest or orientation. For example, in 1986, the Journal of Clinical Child Psychology published an 11 page list describing internship programs offering experiences with children,
youth and families, and The Clinical Neuropsychol-
ogist regularly issues lists of neuropsychology
training programs. Check with faculty members
whose interests parallel yours to determine if they

are aware of similar lists in publications they receive.

Your faculty is another good source of information about internships, although some of their knowledge may be dated. Discuss programs with faculty members who interned at places that interest you or who share your particular clinical interests. In the course of these discussions, you may discover that certain faculty members are personally acquainted with members of the training staff at one or more of the institutions that interest you. If you decide to apply there, it may help to ask these faculty members to send reference letters or call their friends on your behalf. Recommendations from friends and people with whom we are personally acquainted always carry greater weight than those from strangers.

Practical Concerns: Assessing the competition

As you know, Maslow's motivational hierarchy distinguishes survival needs from those that are centered on fulfillment or self actualization. In your reconnaissance so far, you have been focusing on the latter aspect, seeking to identify internships that will enable you to develop to your fullest in a congenial setting. Unfortunately, you won't get fulfilled if you don't get admitted, so it is time we discussed the survival aspects.

Experienced photographers calculate the optimal camera settings to ensure a perfect photograph; they take most of their pictures using that combination, but to be on the safe side, they customarily make some additional exposures above and below that setting.

In applying for internships, you need to do likewise. Most of the programs on your list should be ones that appear to be "just right" for a person with your needs, skills and abilities. But you should also add some that are more competitive in case you have underestimated your marketability, and some that appear easier to get into in the event that the competition is tougher than you expected. You should investigate enough so that, by the time you have finished interviewing and discarded those that you did not like or where you got little encouragement, you have a list of about 10 places with two that you think may be out of reach, five that are just right and three in your safety net.

Making these sorts of estimates involves two sets of calculations. The first is assessing how difficult it is to get accepted into a given program. The second is estimating how strong a candidate you are.

Assessing the programs. How do you determine competitiveness? Unlike college admissions there are no guides to internships rating the difficulty of securing admission. However, there are data available that permit us to make some educated estimates.

As we noted earlier, the APPIC Directory indicates the number of completed applications each program reports having received the previous year. There is no way to determine the accuracy of these figures, and I suspect that programs reporting "100," "200," or "300" applications are using estimates instead of actual counts, but these are the only data available. In the 1990–1991 selection season, the number of applications reportedly received by the 499 APPIC agencies ranged from two to 300 (APPIC 1991a, 1991b). (These are the latest figures currently available. They will be updated annually in the APPIC Directory.)

The Directory also reports the number of positions each program has available. These are broken down into those that are full or half time and funded or unfunded. We will focus on full time, fully funded positions. By calculating the number of applications per position, you can compute a rough index of competitiveness. The internship receiving two applications had three positions available, whereas the one reportedly receiving 300 applications had 16 available. Obviously the latter was more difficult to get into.

As you examine the Directory, you will also notice that some programs have preallocated slots. These are positions that are officially reserved for students from a particular training program and are not available for anyone else. In calculating the competitiveness of a program, you should subtract those positions from the number available, unless of course you are enrolled in the favored training program. Other centers will have slots that are focused on a particular specialty area. For example, one popular program recently noted that six of their 14 slots emphasize geropsychology. That means candidates' chances for acceptance will probably differ depending on whether or not they are interested in a geropsychology position.

In Appendix Two, I have compiled a list of all those internships reporting 100 or more applications in the latest Directory (APPIC, 1991a). Collectively, these 41 programs, having a total of 361 full time, fully funded positions, accounted for 5,504 of the 23,216 reported applications for the 1990-1991 recruiting season (APPIC, 1991b). Because of the sheer numbers, students applying to these facilities probably faced stiffer competition than those applying to less popular programs. This does not mean that it was impossible to obtain one of these slots; indeed, it happened that eight of the 10 Florida State students who applied that year procured positions at these internships.

Assessing your chances. One of the frustrating aspects of evaluating the competitiveness of the internship selection process has been that although the number of positions and the number of applications is reported each year (APPIC, 1991b), until recently there was no way of ascertaining how many actual applicants there are.

85

Although firm figures are still unavailable, we now have some estimates. In 1988, Stedman, Costello, Gaines, Solway, Zimet and Carrington (1990) sent a survey to directors of 272 academic training programs in clinical, counseling and school psychology asking them to project the number of students they would have applying for internship in the academic years 1988/89, 1989/90 and 1990/91. At the time of the survey there were 2,045 slots available in APPIC members' training programs; by 1991 the number had increased to 2,196, 80% of which were APA-accredited (Zimet, 1991).

How many students did the DCTs expect to apply? Stedman et al.'s survey projected totals of 1,966, 2,221 and 2,049 applicants for the three years covered. In short, the overall number of positions slightly exceeded the expected number of applicants in two of the three years. (While the data on the number of slots is firm, the figures on the number of applicants are probably inflated since students and faculty are usually overly optimistic in predicting students' progress.)

Stedman et al. (1990, p. 36) also reported how many applicants could be expected from various types of programs; averaging their data for the three years, it appears that 50.35% of the applicants would be enrolled in traditional APA-approved clinical training programs, 20.19% in APA-approved counseling psychology programs, 8.53% in professional Ph.D. programs, 19.05% in professional Psy.D. programs, and 1.88% from school psychology programs. (Most, but not all, of the programs in the latter categories were APA-accredited.)

Stedman et al. (1990, p. 36) then went on to make the assumption that internships prefer candidates from APA-approved traditional clinical and, to a somewhat lesser extent, counseling programs. Noting that these two categories together constituted only 70% of the available candidates, they wrote, "...if one assumes that the "Preferred" students are those from APA-accredited "traditional" clinical and APA-accredited counseling programs, then one finds a large shortfall."

What does this mean for you? If you are enrolled in an APA-approved clinical or counseling program, it means that you have an advantage because the number of positions available exceeds the supply of candidates.

What if you are not in this preferred group? In the APPIC Directory there is a section with the heading, "Applicants welcome from what programs?" There are six program categories: 1. Clinical, APA-accredited, 2. Clinical, Non-accredited, 3. Counseling, APA-accredited, 4. Counseling, Non-accredited, 5. School, APA-accredited, and 6. School, Non-accredited. Some program directors have indicated that they will only consider applications from certain categories; others have noted which programs are "Preferred" or "Acceptable." The first category, APA-approved Clinical, is universally welcomed; the other five get a varied response.

Place close attention to this section. If many programs indicate that they are not especially enthusiastic over applications from your particular training program, it means you have a smaller pool of potential places to which you can apply. This means you should do everything you can to build up your individual qualifications and credentials. Even if you are not in a clinical program, you may be able to take clinical courses and practica that show you are capable of doing clinical work. Perhaps a year at an unaccredited clinical internship will prepare you for a second year at an accredited facility. In short, you will probably have to work harder and do more to demonstrate to the Selection Committees that you are as good or better than the applicants from the preferred programs. You will also probably have to submit more applications and include a greater proportion of less competitive internships on your list.

Apart from the nature of the program you are in, there are other ways to evaluate your marketability. Being in a preferred program may give you an advantage, but it should not induce complacency. You will still have to work to get the position you want. We have already discussed evaluating your readiness for internship. Other things being equal, the farther advanced you are in your degree program and the more clinical experience you have accumulated, the better your chances will be. I noted earlier the fact that our students have considerably more practicum hours than the APA-stipulated minimum; I am sure that is one reason so many secure positions at highly competitive placements.

Another reason for our success is that previous Florida State students have done well on internship. Their success enhances the reputation of our program and makes it more likely that the internships they attended will be favorably disposed toward future FSU applicants. As I noted earlier, eight Florida State students recently obtained positions at six of the programs which received 100 or more applications that year; two of these programs each enrolled two FSU applicants. All six have had at least one previous FSU student in the last five years, and four had from two to four FSU interns in that period. Does this mean our students are vastly superior to all others? I would certainly like to think so, but I know that, when they were applying, some of these same individuals did not even get invited to interview at some other programs. The internships where we failed to get to first base were typically ones that none of our students had ever attended.

These data demonstrate how academic training programs get "repeated business from satisfied customers." You need to analyze the acceptance and attendance patterns at your school and find out which internships prefer your applicants. If your colleagues have consistently gone to certain training centers and done well, their achievements should enhance your chances of being accepted at those placements. Consider them in forming your list.

The reverse is also true. If you decide to go to some part of the country where no one from your program has preceded you, you may find it more difficult to get accepted. To compensate you might need to submit more applications and apply to more places that appear less competitive. If it is also impossible for you to visit these places personally, so that you will have to rely on telephone interviews, your task will be even more difficult. All of these things that enhance and detract from the strength of your application at different places must be considered when you are formulating your list.

Investigating possible programs

Finally you have completed your list of about 20 internships that interest you, ranging from some that are quite competitive to others where you feel reasonably sure you can gain admittance. For back up, you also have a "lifeboat list" of programs with late due dates in case you need to file some additional applications. These internships should all be ones that you think you might like to attend, but at this stage you know too little about them to be sure. Your next task is to investigate them more closely.

Each Fall, your DCT or training office probably receive brochures from facilities around the country. These are generally mailed after the August APPIC meeting at APA. If a file of these brochures is available, consult it. If not, you and your fellow applicants should volunteer to create such a file. Meanwhile, write to the programs for information and application forms. It is best to wait until September to write to make sure you get the most recent brochure; any earlier and you may get a packet left over from the previous year.

When you write to an internship program, whether you are asking for information or actually applying, it is essential you include all the information on the address you obtained from the APPIC Directory. Many people send their inquiries or applications to the training center without indicating the person or the program for whom it is intended. With thousands of patients and hundreds of staff members from dozens of disciplines passing through a major training center in the course of a year, hospital mail rooms have little time or inclination to deduce who you wanted to contact. A common mistake is for applicants to write to the "Internship program." As Belar and Orgel (1980, p. 672) pointed out, a major consortium may have a number of internship programs in a dozen different disciplines scattered over several hospitals.

As with other aspects of the application process, writing for brochures can be made easier if you have a support group to divide up the work. When you get the brochures and materials, stamp the date on them. Then try to ascertain when they were published. Be wary of brochures that do not have the current year printed on them. Some programs leave their material undated so they can use the same brochure year after year. If so, some of the information, such as staff rosters, may be out of date.

Don't assume accuracy

Remember that the purpose of the brochure, like any other piece of advertising, is to sell you on the internship so you will apply there. Without a pool of applicants, an internship will go out of business. Every year I will be surprised by a large number of students expressing enthusiasm for some program that previous classes had disregarded. When I check the files I usually find that the program in question has just issued a slick new brochure. Be wary about judging a program on the basis of its circulars. As Grace (1985, p. 475) gloomily noted, "The prospective intern should not accept on faith that the internship will meet his or her needs or even that it is primarily designed to do so. Nor should one assume that all information in written and verbal descriptions is accurate. Programs change and misrepresentation is not unheard of." Grace's warning takes on added weight by virtue of the fact that he himself was a Training Director when he wrote his article.

Once you have received your materials, it is time to narrow your list and investigate the most appealing programs in greater depth. Discuss them with faculty and supervisors, especially those who may have interned or visited the site in which you are interested. When possible, talk with fellow students or alumni who may have interned there recently. call

After doing all your homework, you may have some specific questions that will be critical to your application decision. Perhaps you really want a neuropsych rotation, but it is not clear from the brochure whether one will be available this year. Or you may be attracted by the opportunity to work with the famous "Dr. Tibia Femur," but you have heard a rumor that Tibia is leaving the "Brachial Center" and moving to "Humerus Hospital." By all means call the Training Director, or ask your DCT to do so, to check out this information before going to the trouble of applying. Current interns can be an invaluable source of information. Ask for their names and give some a call. When you complete this information-gathering you should have narrowed your list down to about 12 to 15 possible programs.

Some universities require that you get clearance from your DCT or from the training faculty before you may submit any applications. Others may have rules about where you may apply; for example, one university based program reduces inter-student competition by having each student select one first choice and forbidding other students from applying there. Whatever the ground rules, make sure you get your list approved and verify that you have your program's permission to apply to the internships you have selected.

Once you have been cleared to apply and your list has been approved, you are ready to begin the application process. <u>Take your list of sites, with complete addresses, to the Registrar's office and arrange for transcripts to be sent.</u> This is a very low priority item with most Registrars and it can take forever; therefore get your transcripts ordered as soon as possible. Some applicants worry that the transcript may get lost if it arrives before the formal application; others fret that they may change their minds and not apply. Relax; this is the least of your worries. Internship selection committees are well aware that some materials arrive before a formal application is received and they have drawers labeled "Incomplete folders" set aside for that purpose. If you later decide not to apply so the rest of your materials never arrive, they are also skilled at emptying the "Incomplete folders" drawer into the recycling bin after Notification Day.

After you have ordered your transcripts and paid whatever fee is required, it is time to prepare your resume or <u>Curriculum Vitae</u>. This process is described in detail in Chapter Five. And, of course, you will need to prepare your applications. This is discussed in Chapter Six.

get copy for yourself, so you can send unofficial copy + 1ˢᵗ check that it's correct.

CHAPTER FIVE:

PREPARING A RESUME OR CV

The purpose of this chapter is to help you write a successful resume for applying for internship. I use the term "resume" deliberately, because even though you will probably call your resume a "Curriculum Vitae" ("CV" or Vitae for short), the document you will prepare for applying to internship will differ in certain respects from an academic CV.

Your academic CV will focus almost exclusively on scholarship, i.e. your educational history, editorial appointments, professional memberships, and publications, whereas the resume you send to an internship should also include a detailed account of your clinical and professional training, experience, and skills. In addition to listing your various jobs, it should contain a brief description of your duties, the types of patients you saw, the nature and extent of the supervision you received and your competence with various psychometric instruments, items that would be inappropriate in an academic CV. With the understanding that I am not referring to an academic CV, I will use the terms "CV" and "resume" interchangeably in this chapter.

The purpose of your CV or resume is to present a complete and accurate account of all your qualifications in an attractive format that will help you compete successfully with other applicants. This is not the time to be modest. Include all your credentials and relevant experiences.

Every prospective intern I interview has omitted some salient bit of information that will impress some intern directors. Among the most

93

common omissions are professional workshops you may have attended or even presented yourself, undergraduate accomplishments such as graduating with honors, and special skills such as fluency in a foreign language.

While you should not be overly modest, you should not "pad" your CV by listing the same item several times, by including trivia, or by overstating your accomplishments or qualifications. For example, do not list your master's thesis under "education" and again under "publications," or claim expert status on the Rorschach based on five administrations.

Many internships require that you complete a formal printed application form as well as a CV. Since the information that is requested on this will often overlap your CV, I suggest that you begin by assembling all the data you will need for both the resume and the application forms. Next, prepare the resume. Once that is completed, it may be possible for you to answer some of the questions you encounter on the application forms by referring the reader to your CV.

In writing a CV, especially when doing it for the first time, many students get so over-whelmed by stylistic questions they tend to forget the more substantive ones. Should I put my name in the middle or at the side, in regular type or boldface? Should I have it professionally printed? What color paper should I use?

I suggest that you divide the process into four steps and deal with them one at a time as follows:

1. Gather together all the information you will need to complete the CV and the various application forms.

2. From the collected data, select the information you wish to include in your resume.

3. Decide the best way to organize the information you choose to include, i.e. the sequence of topics and what will be listed under each.

4. Present the information in a clear and attractive format. (This is when you decide the stylistic questions.)

Step One: Assembling the information

Writing an initial resume is like filing your income tax...the biggest problem is amassing all the data you may need. In this section I will provide you with a comprehensive list of all the information you should ever need for writing your CV and filling out application forms. In addition, go to the Post Office and obtain "Standard Form 171"; this form is used in all applications for Federal employment including VA internships. It will show you what details regarding education and previous employment you will need to have at hand when you fill out this and other application forms. Whether or not you apply to the VA, fill out your 171 and keep updating it every time you change jobs. Even if you never apply for a federal position, it will serve as a useful repository of information for other applications. Eventually it will be of great assistance to your biographer.

Although I will concentrate on the information you need to assemble for internship applications, as long as you are going to all the trouble of gathering these data, it makes sense to collect and preserve other records you might need when applying for employment or licensing at some future date. Information that seems unimportant now may be essential at some future date, but as the years go by and you move from place to place these data will become increasingly hard to obtain.

As you build up this data bank, don't worry about how to present or display material. That will come later. Just obtain and record the information in whatever manner you find most convenient. I suggest you use a system that will make it easy to add and subtract items and to experiment with different sequences of topics when you get to the organizational phase. You might use a card file or a loose leaf notebook with separate sections for employment, publications and the like with a separate page or card for each item. Most multi-purpose computer software packages include an information storage and retrieval system. Many will allow you to transfer the data to your word processing program. If you elect to store your data on a computer, make sure you back it up on a floppy disk and with hard copy. Make sure you preserve these data, whether computerized or not, in a place that is not only safe but also secure.

The list of information that I will propose is designed to be as comprehensive as possible; there will be many items included that you will not choose to put in your CV. Nevertheless it will be helpful for you to have these data available. Since I am trying to think of everything that anyone might have, there will undoubtedly be many items that do not apply to most readers; do not let this give you a feeling of inferiority.

 Personal information **and** identifying **data.** This information is designed to tell the person who reads your resume who you are and where you can be found. Although you have considerable discretion about how much personal information you wish to disclose, and equal employment opportunity laws place severe restrictions on the information employers can require, for the purpose of assembling a data base I have listed everything you may want or need to include.

1. Name(s): Your complete legal name, including any suffixes such as "Jr." or "III," any former names, especially if you have used them professionally, and any name changes you anticipate between now and Notification Day.

2. Addresses: Record your home and work addresses as well as the address of your

academic training program and the address of someone who will always know how to locate you. Note any anticipated address changes. (Although it is not necessary for internship applications, for some purposes, such as high level security clearances, you may some day need to provide a complete list of the exact street addresses of all the places you have ever lived.)

3. Phone numbers: List the phone and fax numbers associated with the above addresses and the days and times when you can be reached at each, as well as any special information that would be helpful in reaching you, such as "ring ten times to activate the answering machine."

4. Social and demographic information: Include your date and place of birth, Social Security number, marital status, names and birth dates of children and other dependents, your ethnic, racial, or minority status, and your gender if it is not obvious to American readers from your name. If you are not a U.S.citizen, record your citizenship, passport number, current visa status and other relevant data, such as whether you are married to a U.S. citizen.

5. Military status: If you have served in the armed forces, record the branch of the service, your dates of service, medals and honors, discharge status, military serial number, service connected disabilities and/or Purple Heart, and if you are eligible for a Veteran's preference. This information may be especially important if you apply for a VA placement.

6. Legal status: arrests, convictions, probation, parole or imprisonments. (See Federal Form 171).

7. Health: conditions that might have an impact on your ability to perform the duties of your position, i.e. need for a wheelchair accessible workplace.

Education. By and large, for your CV you will only need to list your undergraduate and graduate education noting the degrees and majors, but some of the applications call for lists of courses and dates, so you should get copies of your transcripts and have them available. The more general the application form, such as Form 171, the more likely it is to ask for things such as the number of semester hours or credits you had in your major or minor.

Would-be employers do not ask for GRE scores, but you should keep a record of them in case you apply for admission for further graduate education. In addition to the regular graduate program, you should note all the relevant continuing education courses or workshops you have attended.

1. High school or GED: dates, place etc. (You will not use this in your CV, but some applications may call for it.)

2. Undergraduate education: list every institution attended, noting for each the name of the institution, its address, the dates you attended, your major and minor, any degree you received and the date, and any honors or awards (Cum laude, Phi Beta Kappa etc.). Note any scholarships, awards, achievements, memberships in organizations, extracurricular activities, service on university committees, student government and volunteer activities. Instead of using initials, use the full name of organizations or clubs. If you received an award that is specific to that school, i.e. the "Phineas P. Phollansby Senior Trophy," record what it is for; other readers won't know and after a couple of decades you will forget. If you completed an honors project, record the name of your major professor or advisor and the title of your honor's thesis.

3. Graduate education: For each program attended list the same basic data as above. Have available a transcript for those appli-

cations which inquire about specific courses or numbers of hours. Also include the specific degree program (i.e. APA-approved Ph.D. program in Clinical Psychology), the title of your Master's thesis, major area paper, and dissertation, the name of your major professor(s), your current status (i.e. completed major area paper, candidate for Ph.D.), the date your dissertation prospectus was or will be defended, and the date you anticipate completing your dissertation.

Note any major gaps in your chronology, i.e. periods when you were not enrolled in school or were unemployed, and be prepared to explain them, i.e. raising small children, in a coma, beachcombing, in prison and so on.

4. Other educational experiences:

(a) List professional workshops you have attended, including the person who presented, the date, place and number of hours for each.

b. Technical or professional courses such as computer seminars.

c. Personal therapy or training analysis.

X Special skills. Include knowledge or skills that might be useful in some internship settings.

(1) Languages: list any foreign languages you know and your proficiency level in reading, writing, speaking and understanding.

(2) Special computer skills.

(3) Ability to operate relevant equipment such as biofeedback apparatus.

(4) First aid, or CPR training.

(5) American Sign language for the hearing impaired.

Professional credentials. Include any relevant professional licenses or certificates.

III Professional organizations. List the various professional organizations to which you now belong, or have belonged, with the dates of membership, the level of membership (i.e. student, associate, member, fellow). Include any committees on which you served, and any offices you may have held, such as program chair or nominating committee. Again, do not use initials to identify organizations.

IV Honors and awards. List all of the honors and awards you may have received in college and elsewhere. (When it comes to organizing your actual CV, you can decide whether to list the college awards such as Phi Beta Kappa separately or under "Education"; at this stage redundancy is acceptable.) Include honorary societies such as Sigma Xi, any degrees with honors, and any fellowships or grants. Note offices you have held, both elective and appointed, such as Graduate Student Member on Clinical Training Committee, President of Psi Chi.

If the nature of the honor or award is not obvious, note the name of the organization that presented it and why you received it. If there was a citation, record it verbatim. Later you can decide what details to include. For example, a certain undergraduate fraternity used to present the "American Standard Award" to the brother who spent the most time clutching a toilet as a result of excessive imbibing; if you ever received a similar honor, you probably should ignore my injunction to explain what you did to achieve each award on your CV. In fact, the "American Standard Award" and similar honors, such as being first runner up in the annual Jefferson County Watermelon Festival Seed Spitting Contest, Women's Division, should probably be best omitted.

1. Record exceptional high school awards; i.e. Boy's State Governor; Presidential Scholar Award.

2. Awards from civic or professional organizations, i.e. Lou Brock Leadership Award; APA outstanding first paper award.

Previous employment. In a resume you give a complete employment history, whereas in a CV you typically list only professionally relevant experience. For your internship applications, you will probably strike a balance, including all the positions of a strictly psychological nature and also others that may be seen as tangentially related, such as a weight loss counselor, sleep lab technician or computer consultant, but omitting other jobs, like being a cocktail hostess, that you may have taken to get through school.

In a resume or an application for employment such as Form 171, however, you must list all the jobs you have ever had in chronological order, beginning with your current position and working backward. This usually includes part time as well as full time positions. Don't forget to include military service, especially if your military experience was psychological in nature. At this stage it is a good idea to gather together all the data you will need for both your CV and an application like Form 171.

Preparing a complete employment history is always difficult, especially the first time you do it. Unfortunately, you generally need to submit one for a Federal or state position. If you keep a copy and simply update it as you move from position to position, it is less difficult.

These forms are all similar to one another. Starting with your present position and working backward toward the dawn of time for each and every job you have ever held, list: 1. the name and address of your employer; 2. the dates emloyed; 3. the average number of hours worked per week; 4. your starting and ending salary; 5. the name and phone number of your immediate supervisor; 6. the nature of the business; 7. the exact title of your job, i.e. "Clinical Psychologist III, Step 4"; 8. a description of the work you performed; 9. your specific duties and the percent of time doing each; and 10. your reason for leaving.

These application forms may ask for other information, but, with one exception, all of it is included in the material you have been gathering. The exception is a question asking whether you have ever been fired from any job or quit because you were about to be fired, in which case you then have to go on and supply all the gory details. It is always best to 'fess up and answer these items, and any items with regard to criminal convictions, truthfully and then explain. A positive answer does not bar you from employment, but signing a false application is itself a criminal offense and subjects you not only to dismissal but prosecution for fraud and misrepresentation.

Professional experience. On a CV, in contrast to an employment application, you only include those jobs which are relevant to the position for which you are applying, namely a psychology internship. When you get to organizing your CV, you will probably want to subdivide your experience into two or three categories: research, clinical and teaching. For each, you should provide enough detail to give the reader a clear understanding of the nature of your duties and the extent of your experience.

For each position, you should indicate: 1. the title of the position; 2. the employer; 3. the dates you were employed; 4. the number of hours you worked per week; 5. your specific duties and responsibilities and the percent of time doing each; 6. the name of your supervisor, his or her title and credentials, i.e. "P. Rana Barracuda, Ph.D., ABPP, Supervising Clinical

102

Psychologist (Licensed West Idabama)"; 7. the amount of supervision received weekly and whether it was individual or group. In addition, for future reference it would not hurt to note where each supervisor obtained his or her degree and the year.

The nature of the information you include under "responsibilities" will differ according to whether you are discussing -teaching, research or clinical positions.

1. Teaching: In the case of teaching experience, you should indicate the name and number of the course, its subject matter (i.e. abnormal psychology), the type of course taught (ie. large lecture), the number and the level of students (150 to 200 undergraduates, mostly freshmen and sophomores), and what your role was. Did you have sole responsibility for the course or did you handle the sections and proctor the exams? Do this individually for each course.

2. Research: Indicate the nature of the research and your specific responsibilities, i.e. running subjects, data analysis etc. Cover the specific skills you needed and the techniques you used, i.e. administered SADs interviews to 100 college sophomores.

3. Clinical: Record the type of setting, the nature of the specific clients you saw (age, gender, in or outpatient status, typical problems), and the nature of the contact, i.e. individual or group therapy. Make clear what it is you did in the way of assessment, therapy or whatever and the techniques you utilized. In the case of clinical experiences, record the total number of hours of experience (i.e. 20 hrs. per week for 50 weeks = 1000 hours) and the total number of hours of supervision. At the end of the clinical section include the total number of hours of experience and supervision you will have by the time you report for internship.

a. Summary of experience: Many application forms ask that you produce a small spread sheet or table indicating the number of clients you have seen in various settings and what you have done with them. You may be asked to break down the number of clients by age (children, adolescent, or adults), inpatient or outpatient status, and gross diagnosis, (substance abuse, marital problems, .psychotic etc.). Then you indicate the nature and extent of your contact with the individuals in each group, (i.e. intake, assessment battery, group therapy, individual therapy etc.).

b. Instrument competence: Another frequent request is for a table listing all the assessment instruments that you are familiar with. You may simply be asked to indicate your level of expertise with each or for a more detailed breakdown reporting the number of tests you have administered, scored, or interpreted.

In preparing these tables, you have to walk a fine line between overstating and understating your abilities. People will look askance if you claim "expert" status on the Rorschach after scoring only five, or even 25. On the other hand, don't sell yourself short. There may be some instruments with which you have only a nodding acquaintance, perhaps based on a lecture or a couple of case presentations. It is all right to list "exposure to" these techniques, indicating some familiarity, but not implying proficiency.

In addition to your practicum placements, you may have accumulated additional relevant experience in the course of volunteer work, participating in a telephone counseling service or a crisis management team. List these activities along with dates and salient details such as the type of clients seen, the numbers of hours you spent and the nature of your duties.

Publications and presentations. This is the section that is the core of an academic CV. Most internships will be duly appreciative of your scholarly credentials, as long as they are convinced you can pull your weight clinically. As in previous sections, put everything you can think of into this inventory, then later pick and choose what you will include on your CV. List all items according to the style in the current APA Publication Manual.

1. Articles in refereed journals, including articles already published, those "in press," those being revised   for resubmission, and those under review.

2. Papers at scholarly meetings, posters, symposium contributions etc. in which there is a review for quality. Include those presentations already made and those which are under review.

3. Chapters or contributions to books or monographs that have been published or accepted for publication.

4. Reviews, notes and comments, such as published book reviews, published letters to the APA Monitor or the newsletters of learned societies etc.

5. Unpublished writings, such as your thesis, dissertation, or major area paper, technical reports prepared for granting agencies, as well as training manuals or other internal documents published by your department or employer.

6. Unrefereed presentations, such as colloquia presented to groups of scholars (other than classroom presentations), workshops, staff training presentations at your workplace, creative writing, and film, TV or other media presentations.

suicide
rope
battered 4
depression

Ped 4
Neuro 4
"Career Day"
Counseling Center

Other evidence of scholarly activity.

1. Editorial activities, such as reviewing submissions for a journal or a scholarly meeting, editing or being on the editorial board of a publication such as a journal, a newsletter etc.

2. Grants applied for or received.

3. Consulting activities of a scholarly nature.

4. Summary of current research and plans for future research.

5. Anything else of a scholarly nature you can think of, such as writing software programs.

Miscellaneous. Note any accomplishments or activities not included above that might enhance your resume or help the reader get to know you. Include recreational activities, sports or hobbies, civic service, and non-professional honors, awards, or recognitions such as getting a ribbon in an art show, being elected to office in a civic organization or winning a footrace.

Basic boilerplate. In addition to the data that will form the raw material for your CV and for your applications, there are certain standard questions you are likely to be asked or statements you may wish to include in your cover letter. It may be helpful to prepare them in advance, or at least list the points you will wish to make when these items come up.

1. Who are you? Why did you choose to become a psychologist?

2. What are your goals for the internship?

3. What are your strengths and weaknesses?

(4.) What do you plan to be doing five, ten years from now?

5. Explanations for any potentially embarrassing or puzzling items in your history such as gaps in the chronology, being fired from a job, flunking out of school, or being charged with a criminal offense.

Step Two: Selecting what to include

Once you have assembled all the material you can possibly use, plus a lot more, you can select what information you wish to present in your resume. Since your CV is your creation, there are no formal or explicit rules about what you may and may not include. However, there is a large body of custom and people will generally look askance at those who deviate from the generally agreed upon   format.

One way to steer between the Scylla of appearing to overstate your qualifications or pad your CV with trivial items and the Charybdis of omitting potentially helpful information, is to label items clearly. For example, whereas it is not appropriate to include unrefereed items like grant reports or training manuals under   "Publications," one could include them as "Technical reports (unrefereed)" or "Training manuals." That way they get on the record, but no one can accuse you of misrepresenting these items as refereed publications.

As you scan the material you have assembled, deciding what to put in your CV, you may also note other items that are not appropriate for inclusion in your resume that you will wish to put in a personal statement or cover letter. The "boilerplate" material listed above falls in that category.

Personal information.   Personal information is just that, personal, and it is entirely up to you what to include under "personal" material. You obviously need to list your name, address, and phone numbers.

Information as to marital status and dependents is optional. Female applicants especially have noted a lot of curiosity about their marital status; if it was not indicated on their resume, some interviewers craned their necks to get a glimpse of their ring finger. I have asked TDs about this, and they indicate that the two basic concerns internships have about marital status and dependents is, first, whether marital obligations will have an impact on the likelihood a candidate will accept an offer, and second, whether parental responsibilities will interfere with internship duties. So whether or not you put it in your CV, mention it in your letter or get asked in interview, be prepared to deal with this issue.

If you are married and applying to an internship that involves a major relocation, expect some curiosity about whether your spouse plans to move with you or not. If attending this internship means living apart from your spouse and/ or your children for a year, they may infer that you will be more likely to accept an offer that is closer to home. If this is not the case, you may have to disabuse them of this notion. If you have small children, expect curiosity about who will take care of them and, if you are bringing them with you, whether they will make it difficult for you to put in the necessary hours.

When one of my students who had a small child interviewed at an internship in a distant city, she made a point of telling the interviewer that one of the attractions of that locale was that her aunt who lived there would be able to help her with child care. She got the position.

Realistically or not, there seems to be more concern over relationships for female than for male applicants, and for couples who are married rather than otherwise involved. My advice, which some of my female colleagues say is naive, is to be honest and forthright if you are asked about your plans for your spouse or children. I maintain that if this is going to be a big problem, it is better to find out about it now than after you have started an internship. My female colleagues say, "Get real." You will have to decide for yourself how to handle these issues.

One item I would definitely not include or reveal is the fact that you may be financially secure, especially if you a married woman whose husband is capable of supporting you during your internship. Some places have unfunded positions, and it is my impression that internships are more likely to offer an unfunded slot to "Mrs. Cardiologist," even if she is the best qualified candidate, than they are to other applicants with more limited resources. I have discussed this with women faculty at training centers, and many agree that this can occur.

If you are traveling in tandem and you are both applying to the same place, I would communicate the fact that you are a couple. If you are applying to different programs in the same center, i.e. one to psychology and one to social work, some cooperation between the departments will enhance the chances of your both being accepted. Different institutions in the same locale may also cooperate if they are aware of your situation.

If you qualify as a minority, I would include this information since there are some stipends that are reserved for minority applicants. If you are not a U.S. citizen you may be ineligible for some stipends, so it is best to make this known in advance rather than after you have invested a lot of time and effort in interviewing.

I would not include health or legal status in the CV, but, if there are problems, be prepared to deal with them in interview or on an application form. Concealing relevant information or lying on an application form can not only cost you a job, but could subject you to prosecution. So if you are asked if you have a felony conviction, for instance, answer truthfully.

Education and special skills. Turning to education, do not include high school data on your CV. Do list all the basic information for every college and graduate school attended and your current status in your program. Do not list the courses you have taken; save that for the application form or the transcript. Include the workshops and continuing education seminars you may have attended, but under a separate heading.

Aside from language proficiency, special skills do not generally go in a CV. I would put them in an application or mention them in your cover letter. Do, however, list all your professional organizations and credentials.

When it comes to honors and awards, some discretion is in order. You definitively want to include the important ones, especially those of a clearly professional nature, but do not include others such as being "Hilton employee of the month" or the fact that you won the local pub's wet T-shirt contest. High school awards can be included if they are truly exceptional; the more they relate to professional activities the better, such as winning a major science fair competition.

Previous experience. Under previous experience and employment, include all your relevant professional experience in your CV, but do not put in all the various other jobs you have held. Under "Organizing your CV" I suggest that you subdivide your experience into homogeneous categories such as "research," "clinical" and so on. You do not need to limit this to paid positions; for example you might wish to include a research apprenticeship, even though it was unpaid, under "research experience."

In describing your experience, write clearly and directly, stating what it was that you accomplished. Be forceful; avoid weak, passive or "wimpy" constructions. One university's guide to preparing resumes advises, "Concentrate on the positive and use <u>active</u> verbs in the past tense when stating what you did. To say that you planned, organized, supervised, coordinated, implemented, or designed is far better than saying you were 'involved in' or 'participated in'." (Stanford University Career Planning and Placement Center, 1981, p. 2.) While this advice is aimed at bachelor's level business applicants, you get the idea.

I advise including a table summarizing your instrument competence on your CV, whether or not it is called for in the application form, unless this is one of your weak areas. With regard to other activities, such as volunteer work, you should decide for yourself how significant this activity is and whether it enhances or detracts from your CV. It may be better to allude to it in your personal statement or in your discussion of goals.

<u>Scholarship</u> <u>and</u> <u>publications</u>. Under scholarship, definitely include all your refereed publications and presentations and label them as such. Also include your thesis and, if you have prepared one, your major area paper, but I suggest you list them under "education" rather than as publications. It is appropriate to list items that are under review, but do not put the name of the journal to which they have been submitted. Do not list articles that are "in preparation" under publications. You may refer to them in the describing your future research plans.

In my CV, I have two sections labeled "Notes, reviews and comments" and "Technical reports" in which I include items that have not been refereed. You may wish to include such materials somewhere on your CV as well, but you need to do so in a way that makes it clear you are not trying to "pass these items off" as refereed publications. If you have publications in other areas, such as poetry or short stories, include them in your CV, but list them in a separate section from your psychological writings.

Opinions differ on including sports, hobbies and other non-professional activities. While it may be frowned upon in an academic CV, I do not have any problems with it in a CV designed for internship applications. While some activities, such as being a computer hacker, might enhance the perception of your skills, I think the chief value of such material is that it can help the interview get started or assist you in finding some common ground with the interviewer.

Step Three: Organizing your CV   p 218

Your CV should be organized so that readers can easily find the information they are seeking. A well-organized CV gives the impression that you are a well organized person. The sample CV in Appendix Three will give you some ideas as to organization.

One key is consistency. If you start with your most recent positions and work backwards in the employment section, then you should do likewise in the education section.

I favor putting all the identifying material up front, including demographics, organizations, and credentials. Once this is taken care of, I find it useful to arrange the CV used for internship applications topically. I suggest that you start with the section on education, and put all the information relating to this topic together. Begin with your current status, and then add the information relating to your dissertation (including the title, prospectus date, and major professor) first, followed by your major area paper, followed by your Master's. Include dates to the left. (If you chose to list your masters under "publications," do not list it here as well. However, I think it best to put it here.)

Next summarize your undergraduate education. Include any educational honors you have
received, unless you have chosen to list them
separately under "Honors." (Do not include them
twice, although if you graduated with honors you
should list your bachelors as "A.B., summa cum
laude" or whatever.)

In a separate section, list other educational
items such as workshops. I would also include
skills under this same general heading.

Next, I would present your professional
experience. Rather than putting everything
chronologically, thereby mixing different types of
experience, I prefer to use homogeneous topics
such as "research," "teaching," and "clinical."
The order is up to you and is one way you can
choose what it is you want to emphasize.

Within each section, first list the positions
you have held in reverse chronological order
beginning with the most recent in that topic
area. As noted above, include your title, the
dates, the number of hours worked weekly, the
supervisor, a description of your duties and,
perhaps, the proportion of time spent on each. Do
not include beginning and ending salaries or
reasons for leaving in a CV.

Although you may want to put them in a
separate section, I suggest that you list your
publications immediately after your various research positions. That way everything relating to
research is in one section. Combine any sections
that are too small; i.e. if you have one refereed
publication and two presentations, put them together as "Publications and presentations."

Similarly, in the clinical section, first list all
your positions, then summarize the total number of
hours of experience and supervision. Then I
suggest that you include the table reporting
instrument competence. If you wish, you may add
another summarizing the number and the nature of

the clients you have seen in various settings.

At the end of the CV, you may include a list of the names, titles, addresses and phone numbers of all those you have asked to write letters on your behalf.

Step Four: Style and esthetics

Now that we have dealt with substance, let us turn to style. The most important stylistic issues, overriding all other concerns, is that your resume should be neat, legible, accurate and easy to read.

Your CV will probably be duplicated for distribution to raters at the internship, so use dark, high contrast typography. If you prepare your CV on a word processing system, and you should, use a high quality laser or bubble jet printer rather than a dot matrix. Your department or a copying center should have such equipment available. If you choose to purchase such a printer, it is not necessary to spend a fortune. The camera-ready manuscript for this book was printed on a portable Canon BJ-10e bubble jet printer purchased at a discount store for about $200. Since your CV is going to be handled by a number of people, use a heavy enough grade of paper so that it can stand some wear and tear.

Present the data in such a way that the reader can easily follow the sequence and locate things. Use headings, subheadings and hanging paragraphs to show what belongs with what. Bold face type or different fonts, used judiciously, can also help, but keep it in good taste. A sample CV is provided in Appendix Three.

A common mistake on computer-produced CVs is having an entry carry over a page break. Do not put a heading at the bottom of a page and then have the subordinated material start on the next page, and do not allow a page break to split a job description or reference. If you cannot get it all on one page, it is better to begin the new entry on the next page. Having generous borders and margins is not only attractive, but it also gives the reader a place to make notes.

While you may elect to employ a copying firm, stay away from the outfits that prepare jazzy resumes for siding salesmen. The use of different colored inks, "bullets," raised type and other devices utilized by professional resume firms are fine if you are seeking a sales position, but they are a "turn off" when used in a professional resume or CV. Similarly, it is not customary to include a photograph on a CV.

Helen

No matter how many times you have gone over it, before you take your CV or any other material to be copied, check for typos. Check everything again when you get it back from the copying firm; do not accept it if there are dark spots or slanted pages. Make sure you check every copy...the one you do not check will be the one with the blank page.

This may seem very basic, but all of these mistakes have been made in the past. Even one error or botched page can give a very negative impression. I recently read a job application in which the candidate spelled the name of his home state incorrectly. The fact that the applicant had obviously not bothered to check a document as important as a job application for accuracy made me wonder if he could be trusted to analyze data or prepare research articles correctly.

Mistakes are especially likely to happen when you rely on others to prepare or copy your materials. I speak from experience; before we submitted the manuscript for the first edition of this book, four different people had proofed it in its entirety. However, the cover was prepared at the print shop; I simply supplied the drawing. When I received my copies from the printer, I looked at the cover and saw that my name had been spelled incorrectly! The books had all been printed and it was too late to correct it. However, it certainly was an effective illustration of my point that no matter how careful you are, mistakes happen. Let's hope that the printer gets my name right in this edition, and that you get your CVs right before you mail them to the internships.

CHAPTER SIX:

PREPARING YOUR APPLICATIONS

Once you have formulated your priorities, compiled your list of possible internships and prepared your CV, it is time to prepare your applications. Allow plenty of time, because this will take longer than you think. Let us begin by reviewing the steps you should have completed by now.

Before you actually submit any applications, make absolutely sure that you have satisfied whatever requirements your department may have for internship applicants. While some programs allow students to apply whenever they feel they are ready, others have a formal procedure involving a transcript check, approval by the DCT or even, as in our program, a vote by the full Clinical Faculty.

Your department may also have an established procedure for submitting applications. You may be expected to meet with your DCT, or have your CV and other materials reviewed before you send anything off. Whatever the system is in your department, make sure you follow it to the letter, even if it differs from the advice in this book. You do not want to get a reputation for being a loose cannon just at the time you are asking faculty members to write letters saying how cooperative and responsive to supervision you are.

Let us assume that you have gotten whatever clearance is necessary and have discussed your choices with your advisors. It is now late October or early November and you should have:

1. Compiled a list of places where you plan to apply.

File folders + "milk carton"

2. Obtained application forms from all of those places.

3. Collected all the information you need to complete the application forms.

4. Prepared a CV or resume, had it laser printed and duplicated.

5. Had transcripts sent to all the places where you might conceivably apply.

6. Provided your DCT, major professor, and professional supervisor(s) with complete addresses of the people to whom they are to send letters of recommendation and requested that they get them all in the mail prior to the Thanksgiving break.

As I noted in Chapter Four, some students worry that transcripts and letters which arrive before the formal application materials are received may go astray. Don't. Every year at this time all the internship training centers all over the country start receiving application materials. As soon as an item comes in, they check their data base and see if they already have a listing for that person. If so, the material is added to the file; if not, a file is opened and subsequent material is inserted as it arrives. Since it often takes the Registrar's office a long time to process a transcript request, and since faculty members may put off writing letters of reference, the safest procedure is to request these materials early, even if you have not yet submitted your formal applications.

You will also note that different training centers have different due dates, typically ranging from the end of November until the middle of January. If time is short, prepare those with the earliest due dates first, submitting each application as soon as it is ready. However, since most of your references will send the same basic letter to all your sites, it is best to give them the complete list all at once so they can mass produce their letters.

Where to apply

Now it is time to bite the bullet and actually decide where you are going to apply and how many applications to submit. As I indicated earlier, your list should include settings that range in competitiveness. By all means apply to those places you are really enthused about, but, if they are very competitive, also apply to some other places that are less popular. Your final selection should include facilities that range from being highly competitive to relatively noncompetitive.

While you are deciding on the internships that should be on your final list, flag some others for a "lifeboat list." These should be internships you would be willing to attend, but which for some reason you are less interested in applying to than the others. All should have relatively late due dates. — backc-ups

As the name implies, the "lifeboat" list is for emergencies. You will probably never need it, but, if you do, it can save your life. You use your lifeboat list if, midway through the application season, you discover some disaster has wiped out your primary list or a number of places thereon. This is the backup list you turn to if you only applied to internships in Los Angeles and the "big" earthquake some have predicted hits a month later, flattening everything west of the San Andreas Fault.

You have enough anxieties without my reciting the various reasons why you might be forced to submit additional applications late in the game. In the one instance where we had to use a lifeboat list, a good student got a poorly phrased letter of recommendation that threatened his chances for acceptance at his primary list. He went through with interviews, but on my advice submitted five additional applications (with a more appropriate letter) to his backups. After interviewing, one of his backups actually became his first choice and he was accepted there.

Many internships have separate tracks such as child, substance abuse, forensic, and gerontology. In some of these settings, the applications are sorted according to the track specified and candidates are considered by the subset of faculty with whom they will be working. Therefore, it is vital that you clearly indicate what track you are applying for in such programs.

Although other internships may not have track-specific selection, they often must ensure that all their major rotations are covered. The interests expressed by the applicants may be an important selection criterion. Thus, you should be sure your preferences are clearly indicated.

Do not make frivolous applications. This is no time to indulge in ego trips. Do not apply to famous places you have no intention of attending simply to see if you could get in. You may interfere with the chances of other students who are seriously considering the site in question. Also, do not apply to nearby facilities "for practice" so you can use them to test your interviewing technique even though you have no plans to attend. This will give all applicants from your institution a bad name and may interfere with the chances of your fellow students who are tied to the area and who may be very interested in those sites. The bottom line is, "Do not apply any place you are not willing to attend." It is not only a waste of your time and the internship's, but in my opinion it is dishonest.

Whether or not your program requires it, you should try to coordinate your applications with those of your fellow applicants. It is all right for two or three people from a single university to apply to the same internship. It is not uncommon for internships to accept two candidates from the same program, although most would balk at three. After interviewing it is likely that each applicant will end up with a different first choice. Some internships resent getting too many applications from the same school (Belar & Orgel, 1980). Recently, one facility received a carton containing two dozen applications from one school. Apparently, identical cartons had been sent to a number of major training centers, with no attempt to match the individual applications to the resources of the facilities. The TD sent the carton back by return mail with instructions for the DCT to select and submit the best application for her internship.

How many applications should you submit?

Plan to submit a reasonable, but not an excessive, number of applications. What is a reasonable number of applications? This varies with the competitiveness of the internships to which you are applying, the strength of your training program, the number of your fellow students applying to the same internships, your credentials, and whether you are applying in tandem with someone else.

Perhaps you are enrolled in one of the "less preferred" training programs discussed in Chapter Four, such as one that is not APA-accredited. If so, you will need to submit more applications than someone from a stronger program, and you will have to target them to centers that are more receptive to such candidates from such programs. If you are an average student, you should apply to more places than if you are the class superstar, especially if you are applying to the same places as the superstar.

Popular internships which receive a large number of applications, such as those listed in Appendix Two, are always risky, no matter how strong a candidate's credentials. I never sleep well when my students apply to such programs, even though we have a good record with some. If one or more of these programs is at the top of your list, you should have plenty of backups. You usually will have a better chance applying to training centers with which your university has strong traditional ties than one which has never before taken a student from your school. Within internships, child and psychotherapy tracks seem to draw a much greater proportion of applications than other slots such as chemical dependency or gerontology.

In deciding how many applications to submit, be prepared to delete a couple of possibilities after you visit, because you will undoubtedly find one or more unacceptable for some reason. For example, one of our students who had obviously not done his homework very well submitted an application to a VA Hospital that did not even have a Psychology Training Program! If circumstances will prevent you from interviewing in person, submit more applications. Even though they may say telephone interviews are acceptable, many programs favor candidates they have actually seen. As noted above, you should apply to some less competitive as well as some more competitive internships, and it is a good idea to have a "lifeboat list" tucked away in case it suddenly becomes necessary to submit some additional applications at the last minute.

In terms of actual numbers, I have had students submit as few as one application and as many as 26. All in all I now recommend 12 +/- 2 applications. This is one more than I recommended in the first edition of this book, because it seems to me that the competition is getting tougher. (Perhaps it is due to all the applicants that are using this book.) In any event, if the number of candidates continues to increase over the years, you may need to prepare more applications.

This number is consistent with the national average of 11.6 applications for each fully funded APA-approved position (APPIC, 1991b). However, an intern participating in a symposium at the 1989 APA Convention stated that she had been one of

122

40 students applying from a freestanding Psy.D. program and that she and her classmates had averaged 22 applications each. This is twice the number I recommend, but we have far fewer students applying each year, and our program is one of those that is considered "preferred" since it is a traditional APA-approved Ph.D. program in clinical. Ultimately, you must decide what is the best number for you to submit; for many applicants deadlines and fatigue are the final determinants.

Preparing your applications

When you prepare and submit applications, make sure you comply with the application procedures specified by each program. Failure to do so will show that you do not know how to follow directions, and no one wants a trainee who cannot or will not follow directions.

Formal applications. Many programs will send you a printed application form for you to fill out. If you are accustomed to using a word processor, it will be very frustrating to revert to a typewriter. Order a large bottle of correction fluid and a paint roller. According to May, Rice and Birckhead (1990), some internships have moved toward standardizing their application forms. The Association of Psychology Internship Training Agents (ACCTA) has developed a standardized form that combines a number of items TDs have found useful. The more the application forms are standardized, the more you may be able to utilize word processing technology, since it will be more cost effective to enter a standard form onto your computer.

However, many programs are reluctant to standardize their forms or to make the application process any easier. Why? If you were on the Selection Committee of a program receiving 100 or more applications, you, too, might resist changes that could encourage even more candidates to apply. May et al. (1990, p. 38) reflected many internships' dissatisfaction with such applications when they wrote, "The advent of the word processor has led to 'mass produced' applications that are frequently not very revealing....Disadvantages [of standardized application forms] include a tendency to homogenize applicants and a possible increase in applications from candidates who are not serious but wish to 'hedge their bets'."

In filling out applications, follow directions but do not get too obsessive about it. If the form provides only two inches for a response and you need three, especially if it asks you to list all the honors you have received, then add a continuation page. Some applicants reduce the type size to make it fit by selecting smaller fonts on a word processor or by using a duplicating machine in reduction mode; you can try these maneuvers if you choose, but you should ask yourself if it is really worth all the extra time and effort required.

After reading dozens of similar responses, reviewers take note when one turns up that has some originality or humor. Late one night, a student who had been preparing applications all day encountered a form that asked him to "list his strengths." He impulsively wrote down, "I have never been arrested," and went on to the next item. After he had mailed the applications, he regretted his flip answer and figured he could write off that placement. To his surprise, when he interviewed everyone at the agency was eager to meet the one intern applicant with a sense of humor, and he was treated like visiting royalty. (Of course, if you all start using his response, it won't appear original any more.)

You will find that some application forms are unbelievably complicated and time-consuming to prepare. "Why," you might ask, "do they need all this information?" They don't. Extremely complex applications are a test of your motivation, designed to screen out anyone who is not a serious applicant.

Personal statements and essays. Because of their dissatisfaction with the information contained in application forms and letters of recommendation, many programs will also ask you to submit a personal statement or essay. Typical topics include a mini-biography ("Who are you?"), a discussion of why you want to be a clinical psychologist, an essay on why you want to attend their particular internship, or a statement on what you plan to be doing after you get your degree.

It is up to you to prepare your own essays. I suggest that you be positive, realistic and professional and avoid using the statement as a [not] confessional. I have read the sort of applications that begin, "It was only after I accepted the fact that I am an alcoholic and that I had ruined the lives of my family that I realized I had been chosen to save others by becoming a clinical psychologist." I am rarely eager to hire such people.

In addition to the personal statements, one internship is reported to be experimenting with an addendum to their standard application which asks candidates to prepare responses to questions in the areas of professional ethics, assessment and interventions that are modeled after state licensing examinations (May et al., 1990). If this catches on, applications will include what amounts to a take home examination.

In addition to being a test of your motivation, essays and personal statements are evaluated on the basis of style and literacy as well as actual content. Writing is an important part of any psychologist's job, and these compositions show raters whether you can write clearly and cogently. Make sure you revise and edit these essays, and check them for style and spelling.

Work samples. Some programs may request that you submit a clinical work sample, typically an assessment. If a work sample is requested, I suggest you determine how absolute this requirement is. It may do you more harm than good. I was surprised to learn from one internship director whose hospital supposedly requires a work sample that applicants who do not submit one are not penalized. In fact, he noted, it seemed to work the other way -- the students who did submit work samples tended to draw more negative ratings from faculty because they had something concrete to criticize! I have raised this issue with other directors and they concur.

A request for a work sample can also raise ethical issues. If, during your reconnaissance, it appears likely that a work sample will be required, your safest course of action is to perform an evaluation expressly for your application, using a competent volunteer who has had the purpose of the assessment explained, given informed consent, and signed a release that will allow you to share the data and the report, suitably disguised, with internship selection personnel. Not only will this permit you to select a battery that will best highlight your skills, but it should also enable you to avoid some of the ethical dilemmas that have plagued others.

This procedure avoids some of the ethical difficulties associated with seeking an after-the-fact release from a client you have previously evaluated. One student felt that obtaining such a release would violate his understanding with clients he had previously assessed, so he asked if he could substitute a report he had prepared for a class on projectives using materials provided by the instructor, who had procured them from a consenting client. Although most TDs understood his concern and allowed the substitution, one insisted that he provide a work sample with tests he had administered personally. This led the student to question that TD's sensitivity to ethical issues and, eventually, to withdraw his application at that program.

Cover letters. Although no agency will list this as a requirement, by all means include a one-

Good Bond paper
beige/cream

page cover letter. This cover letter will be the first thing the reviewers read, and it is vital to making a good first impression.

The cover letter gives you a chance to emphasize the points you are trying to make in your resume and personal statement. Indicate who you are, what position you are applying for, what is included in your application, whose letters of reference they can expect to receive and, in a couple of sentences, why you are applying to this program and why they should select you. This is one sure way to make your application stands out from all the rest, especially since many of your competitors won't bother to send any cover letter.

It is much easier to submit the same cover letter and personal statement to all your internships. It is also less effective. Adapt your cover letters and personal statements to each individual internship, indicating the specific people and programs that attract you and why you feel there is a good match between your abilities and needs and what the program offers. Of course, it requires a lot more work to individualize your applications. But everyone wants a hardworking intern.

Remember, most selection committees are faced with the task of selecting a small number of outstanding and congenial people from a large number of applicants, most of whom are qualified. Unless an application catches their attention from the start, there is little incentive to wade through it all or to invite the applicant for an interview. Raters are most likely to notice applicants who have done their homework and whose letters and personal statements show they are familiar with the program and how it meshes with their qualifications. Many internships will make their first selection based only on your application materials. If you don't make the cut, you don't get invited for an interview.

Spelling and style. Until and unless you are

selected for an interview, your application is you. Make sure it is complete, clean, and correct. Sloppy applications suggest you have sloppy standards. Check for typos and misspelled words. Do not rely on your computer to catch spelling mistakes. A spell-checking program will approve both "form" and "from" even though one will be incorrect in a given context; you do not want to report that you are familiar with the Revised From (sic) of the MMPI.

Unrequested materials. Determine program policy about submitting unrequested materials, such as reprints, prospectuses or copies of term papers. If you have a published reprint, I would definitely include it, but I would hesitate at a typewritten preprint that makes the folder bulky, and I would not include academic papers unless specifically told to do so.

Unless you are required to submit a clinical work sample, I would not do so. A clinician can always find something to criticize in someone else's work sample. If there is a perceived flaw, you will get marked down. If it is flawless, they will assume your supervisor is responsible. Either way, it is a no-win situation.

Letters of recommendation

Most internships agree that letters of recommendation are of little help in selecting candidates (May, Rice & Birckhead, 1990). Since applicants select most of the letter writers, they are hardly objective. The letter writer's goal is to help get the applicant admitted rather than to provide a candid appraisal. As a result, the letters received are overwhelmingly positive, prompting some writers to ask whatever happened to the lower 90% of the student population (May et al., 1990; Miller & Van Rybroek, 1988). May et al. (1990, p. 39) concluded, "...training directors will only see letters as informative if they 'damn with faint praise.' Letters are apparently used more often to lower an applicant's ranking than as a general discrimination factor."

I disagree. As DCT, I spend a great deal of time on composing each student's letter. I begin by reviewing the student's transcript, CV, academic folder and my notes of my interviews with the applicant regarding internship. I read all the letters of recommendation sent by undergraduate mentors prior to admission at FSU, and the quarterly ratings made by clinical supervisors, noting quotations I can use in my letter.

I then integrate all this information into a three- or four-page summary of the candidate's individual characteristics. This is descriptive rather than evaluative, although I do my best to put things in a positive light. For example if a candidate has been in the program for an eternity, I emphasize his maturity and experience, whereas one who is applying early and has relatively few hours is praised for her youthful energy and drive. If there are deficits, I acknowledge them and try to explain what the problem was. TDs can forgive candidates for some bad grades if they know they were ill or going through a divorce at the time and the problem is now resolved. Whenever possible, I try to include concrete behavioral examples to illustrate points made in my evaluation.

TDs often report that they find these individualized letters are helpful in evaluating candidates, especially when they are attempting to compare several applicants from our program. Since our candidates appear to do pretty well, these frank appraisals evidently do not hurt their chances perhaps because the information is accurate and placed in context.

Who to solicit for letters. You should submit at least three letters of recommendation. One should be from your major professor, one should be from a clinical supervisor and one must be from your DCT. Only solicit letters from people with appropriate professional credentials who are in a position to evaluate your skills as a psychologist. Character references from clergy or civic leaders have no place in an internship application.

(1) Your major professor's letter should focus on your academic qualifications and research. In addition to all the other good things your major professor discusses, there must be a statement *Eileen* that you will definitely finish your dissertation and obtain your doctoral degree in the foreseeable future. No one wants an intern who will be an "ABD."

I ask our major professors to evaluate students in absolute rather than relative terms. I prefer a letter that says a student is "excellent" to one that says he or she is the "best." The reason is that comparative statements implicitly put down other students from our program who may also be applying. If I have two or three major professors each claiming his or her student is the "best," or even in the "top 5%," they all lose credibility. (You and I both know that a large proportion -- perhaps even 50% -- of the students who apply each year are actually below the median, but not according to any of the letters that will be written.)

(2) The second letter should be from someone who is familiar with your clinical work. This should be someone who has supervised you recent- *Cyd ?* ly rather than in the distant past. If you have *Marty* had recent experience in a couple of different set- tings, it is a good idea to have letters from both. Before listing anyone as a reference, make sure you ask their permission. If someone does not feel comfortable in recommending you, or is going to be away when the letters are due, it is better to find out early and obtain other references.

(3) The third letter must be from your DCT. This is the program's formal endorsement of your application, and it certifies that you are a student *Cynthia* in good standing who is academically and clinical- ly prepared for internship. While I provide a very

thorough appraisal, I am told that many DCTs' letters are relatively brief and simply state that the candidate has the program's blessing.

Other letters. In addition to these three "must" letters, it is wise to solicit a fourth "wild card" letter as well, preferably from someone who thinks you are terrific. This letter can help balance a perfunctory DCT letter or one from someone who for some reason "damns you with faint praise." It can also fill in if one of the others is late arriving. Some programs may not evaluate any folders until there are at least three letters; your "wild card" letter will allow it to go forward without delay.

You may be applying to some places where someone on your faculty has a "special relationship" with one or more members of the staff. Perhaps they were colleagues some place, or maybe your faculty member was the staffer's major professor. In such instances, it may help to have that faculty member write or call his or her friend on your behalf. Check first with your DCT, and do not ask a faculty member to make a special appeal on your behalf unless you are very interested in that setting. If, after such a call, you decide not to attend that internship, it will be embarrassing for both your faculty member and his or her friend.

The reciprocal situation is when some old time faculty member, like our mythical "Prof. Muledeer," assures you that, if you give the word, a single phone call to his former student, "Dr. Carrie Boux," will ensure your acceptance at "Moosehead Medical Center." If this occurs, thank the good professor and check with your DCT. If Moosehead is your first choice, and your DCT approves, you may decide to let Prof. Muledeer call. However, do not burn your bridges to other training centers.

Recently, our version of "Prof. Muledeer" heard that one of his graduate students, let us call her "Fawn Doe," was applying to "Moosehead Medical Center," and he offered to intervene on her behalf. Unfortunately, he swore her to secrecy because I might get upset. Ms. Doe agreed, and soon after he assured she would definitely get a slot at Moosehead. Fawn took Prof. Muledeer at his word; when TDs from other internships called her, she thanked them for their interest and told them she planned to accept the offer that would be forthcoming from Moosehead.

There was one slight problem, however. The younger stags had taken over at Moosehead and, a week before Notification Day, Fawn was informed she was out of the running. By the time she finally came to me, she had almost destroyed her chances of acceptance elsewhere. With a lot of abject phone calls to other TDs, we managed to get her into another Appendix Two program, albeit not in her preferred rotation. Muledeer was right about one thing, however; I definitely was upset. The moral of the story is that you should always keep your DCT informed.

Submitting your applications

Finally you have all your application materials completed. For each application you should have an individualized cover letter, a copy of your CV, completed application forms, personal statements or essays, work samples if required, and any other material you are submitting, such as reprints.

Next assemble each individual application. Make sure that each is complete and correct, accurate and attractive. Make certain that you have the right materials in each application. If you have prepared individualized cover letters or personal statements, as I have suggested, make sure they are going to the correct place. It will not help your cause if the extremely behavioral internship gets the letter in which you express your interest in dynamic psychology and in learning more about Rorschach interpretation, while the analytic institute receives the statement indicating you hope to become a radical behaviorist. Similarly, double-check your addresses, and make sure the name of the training director matches the internship, and the address on the envelope matches the one inside. Finally, don't forget to sign the letters.

After you have sealed each completed application, take them personally to the Post Office, have them weighed, put on the correct postage and send them off. If application dates remain the same, you should send them all off by the day before Thanksgiving. Then you can relax and enjoy the holiday.

Following up

It is your responsibility to ascertain that your application has been received by the internship facility and is complete. (Some programs will request that you include a stamped self-addressed postcard for this purpose.) After a reasonable time has passed to allow the applications to be logged in and filed, check to make sure your application is complete and all your letters of recommendation have been received.

Don't get annoyed if the internship staff is not able to give you an immediate answer as to whether or not some vital document has been received. Remember that APPIC reported that 23,216 applications were received in 1990-1991. If each application involved at least seven documents (cover letter, transcript, application form, CV and three letters), that means that over 160,000 documents had to be filed in over 23,000 folders in a two-month period that includes the Thanksgiving, Christmas and Chanukah holidays Moreover, you are not the only person calling. This is why so many Training Directors and their staffs get so hassled every winter. If they can't find something right away, don't get hysterical. If you make yourself truly obnoxious to the harried clerical staff, someone may make sure that your folder really does get lost and that it stays lost. It is one way to make sure you won't be bothering them all next year.

When you get an answer, if you find your folders are complete, tell them that you hope to interview, and start working on your travel plans. If you are told your folder is incomplete, don't panic. Perhaps the training center has misfiled something. This is especially likely if you have changed your name. Your transcript will probably have your former name while you are using your new name. If you use a hyphenated name, such as "Eggs-Benedict," have them look under "B" as well as "E." Similarly, if you have an Hispanic name such as "Guillermo Huevos Rancheros" and you go by "Huevos," see if some material has been filed under "Rancheros." An Asiatic name such as "Egg Foo Young" could lead to materials being filed under "E," "F," or "Y," depending on how knowledgeable the clerk is with regard to Eastern customs. Finally, if you have a fairly common name, such as "Jim Smith," it is possible that more than one person with your name has applied, and some of your material may be in the other person's folder.

Assuming the missing material cannot be located, take steps to resubmit it. You should have copies of all the material you submitted. If a letter is missing, find out if it was ever written or mailed; if so, have a duplicate copy sent. If not, get on the party's case. Find out how urgent the time constraints are, and fax or Federal Express material if necessary. (If it is a small document, fax is cheaper and faster.)

You may be told that it is too late and that nothing more will be accepted. Send it anyway, then ask your DCT to call the TD or, failing that, call the TD yourself. Messages like this are usually the result of overzealousness or misunderstanding on the part of a lower echelon clerical person. TDs, on the other hand, do not wish to offend any university training programs unnecessarily.

If even this does not work, thank the powers that be you have discovered how rigid and autocratic that place is. You certainly would not have enjoyed interning there! Remember, you agreed back in the Foreword to this book that no internship is worth pursuing as if it was the Holy Grail. Moreover, you have just saved yourself some travel money. To save more, proceed to the next chapter.

Copy e/x in app.

NOTES

CHAPTER SEVEN:

TRAVELING TO INTERNSHIPS:

HOW TO SURVIVE AND STAY SOLVENT

Your next step is visiting the internships to which you have applied and interviewing. I am a firm believer in the importance of the on-site interview. Although it may not be required, I feel it enhances your chance of being accepted. More important, however, is the fact that it affords you an opportunity to evaluate a setting and its personnel before deciding if you want to spend a year of your life training there.

Chapter Eight deals with the interview process. We will discuss internships' interview policies, how to arrange for interviews, and, most important, what to do, say and ask during the interview itself. This chapter focuses on travel; if you cannot afford the trip or if you get stranded en route to the internship, all the interview skills you have acquired will be wasted.

Travel is the biggest single expense associated with applying for internships. It can also be a major hassle. The purpose of this chapter is to help you save time and money traveling to internship sites and to maximize your chances of actually getting to your intended destination on or about the time you planned, with your luggage and your temper intact. This despite the fact that you will be traveling at the worst time of the year from the standpoint of air fares, weather and crowds.

In the pages that follow, I will offer a great deal of unsolicited advice, most learned the hard way. Unfortunately, this will also make me sound like your mother.   However, if you want to save money, avoid hassles and stay healthy on the road, heat up a cup of chicken soup, find a comfortable chair and get out your highlighter.

Join the club(s)

As soon as possible join the frequent traveler programs of the major airlines you are likely to be using, the AAA automobile club, and the preferred guest programs of the major hotel chains. The AAA charges an annual fee, most of the others are free.

The main purpose of the airlines' frequent traveler programs is to build customer loyalty by rewarding you for flying with them. The more you fly, the more "frequent traveler miles" you earn; these "miles" can later be redeemed for upgrades or free travel. You typically get a bonus of several thousand "miles" for joining, and then at least 500 to 1000 miles credit for each "flight segment." For example, on a generous airline, if you fly from Charleston, SC to Chicago, IL and back, changing in Atlanta, you can accumulate four "flight segs" or 4,000 miles. If you fly to San Francisco, again changing in Atlanta, you may get 1,000 miles for the Charleston to Atlanta flight seg, and the actual mileage (2,139) for the Atlanta to San Francisco segment. The total round trip "miles" would be 6,278. Combined with your bonus for joining, on one airline this would give you enough miles for an upgrade to first class on a subsequent round trip. On that same airline, as few as 15,000 miles can be redeemed for an off-peak companion ticket and 20,000 can earn an off-peak round trip coach ticket anywhere in the United States. Other airlines give fewer points and "charge" more miles for premiums.

The basic mileage credits are just the beginning. Promotions occur which will award you double or triple mileage if you travel through certain cities, fly at certain times, stay at certain hotels, or pay for your travel in certain ways. In addition to rewarding you with free travel coupons after you accumulate enough miles, the frequent traveler programs also entitle you to reduced rates at cooperating hotels and car rental agencies. Their monthly publications also announce special discounts and bargains that might help you save money.

Like air fares, the amount of incentive points awarded and the amount needed for various rewards waxes and wanes. Airlines that are having trouble attracting passengers may offer more incentives. If they fold, however, you lose the benefits. When I was traveling extensively while preparing the first edition of this book, the good news was that I accumulated 500,000 miles, enough for a couple of trips around the world; the bad news was that it was all on Eastern Airlines which soon went bankrupt.

The AAA automobile clubs do more than provide emergency road service. They will give you free tour books listing hotels and motels and their rates in the places you will visit, and will also supply you with free state and city maps that will help you find your way from the airport to the training center. An AAA card also entitles you to discounts at major car rental agencies and many hotels. They also provide travelers' checks free of surcharge.

Most hotel and motel chains also have their own travel clubs. These include the Marriott "Honored Guest" program, the Hilton "Honors," the Holiday Inn "Priority Club," the Radisson "Key Rewards," the Hyatt "Gold Passport" and even the Days Inn "Inn-Credible" Card Club. Some, like Hyatt, charge an annual fee; others such as Holiday Inn, assess a one-time initiation fee. Most are free.

Compared with the airlines programs, the hotel and motel preferred guest programs take a considerable time (and expense) before you build up enough credits to qualify for an award such as a free weekend. They typically give you a point for every dollar you spend. You may prefer to have the credits applied to your airline account. Their main value is that they often entitle you to certain perks such as an "800" number for improved reservation service, a special check-in line, discounts, free breakfast, a room upgrade, or a morning paper.

Saving money on air travel

As you know, since deregulation, air travel costs can vary wildly and seem to have no rational basis. Most travelers are accustomed to costs being based on mileage... the longer the trip the more it costs. Not so in air travel. I once flew from Tallahassee, FL to Toronto, Ontario for less than it had cost me to fly from Tallahassee to Fort Myers, FL the previous week. The overhead involved in air travel... salaries, gate rental, insurance, aircraft...is so high that once the airline gets a plane in the air, the distance it flies is a negligible aspect of the total cost.

Instead, air prices are driven by the need for the airlines to fill as many seats as possible to break even. Thus, they will offer all kinds of inducements and discounts to fill the empty seats on the less popular flights, while charging the highest fares possible on the heavily subscribed routes. This leads to some strange paradoxes. For example, the fare from San Francisco to Dallas, a very popular route, is $360, but there is a cheap flight from San Francisco to Kansas City, changing in Dallas, for $195 (Gavzer, 1992). Book the Kansas City flight, carry your luggage, get off at Dallas and pocket $165.

Or you may discover that the whole is greater than the sum of its parts. Gavzer (1992) reports that while a direct full-fare ticket from Los Angeles to Dallas may cost $330; by taking the cheapest flights from LA to Albuquerque ($95) and from Albuquerque to Dallas ($92), you can make the trip for $187, thus saving $143. This "split city" scheme is terrific if you want to visit an internship in Albuquerque; otherwise you may waste a lot of time there waiting for your cheap flight to Dallas.

It is essential that you consult a knowledgeable expert who is willing to work with you to take full advantage of differential fares and discount rates. Remember, travel agents work on a commission. For them, time is money. So the more time they spend saving you money, the less they make. A good one who values your repeat business and enjoys finding you a bargain can be very helpful, but do not expect that every one will automatically give you that level of service. Ask around and shop for a good agent.

If you are a fairly sophisticated computer user, have a modem, and subscribe to a personal information system or "gateway" such as Prodigy, Genie or Compuserve, you can be your own travel agent. You can access American Airlines' "EAASY SABRE" system, see for yourself what flights are available at which fares on the date you wish to fly, and make your own reservations. You can also choose how to receive your tickets. A nice feature of the system is you can request it to present you with the options available according to the fares, beginning with the least expensive.

Whether you use your computer or a travel agent, be prepared to invest a fair amount of time and effort planning your trip to obtain the lowest prices. For example, I recently had a meeting in Chicago, so I decided I would use the occasion to visit one of our students who was interning at the University of Rochester School of Medicine. Looking at the map, it seemed it would be easy to fly from Tallahassee to Rochester, NY, visit the intern, fly on to Chicago, attend my meeting, and return home. Not so. Thanks to the "hub" system, none of the airlines serving Tallahassee flew from Rochester to Chicago; I could go to Rochester and return from Chicago on an "open jaws" plan for about $500, but getting from Rochester to

Chicago on another carrier would cost $350 for a total of $850.

Since one usually saves money by staying with a single carrier, I tried again, plotting a zigzag route that had me going from Rochester to Chicago via the hub in Cleveland. That pushed the total to over $1,000. It seemed I would have to abandon my plan to visit Rochester, so I asked the round trip fare from Tallahassee to Chicago; $168 I was told. On an impulse, I asked the round trip fare from Chicago to Rochester and return on the other carrier and found it was only $178. That's right, they charged $178 round trip, but $350 one way! Apparently many more people want to go from Rochester to Chicago than vice versa. So, by buying one round trip from Tallahassee to Chicago and another round trip from Chicago to Rochester, I was able to do the whole trip for $346 instead of the $850 I was first quoted. Although I saved $500, it required a least a half a day to work everything out.

As a general rule you can save a great deal by booking early and paying promptly, but you often must pay a penalty of as much as 100% if you cancel or make any changes. For example, recently the unrestricted round trip coach fare from my home city to Los Angeles was $1,020, the restricted excursion with a 25% penalty ranged from $400 to $460, and the restricted excursion with a 100% penalty was $350 to $410 depending on the time of day and so on. However, if I made my arrangements properly, I could stop off at Dallas or Houston for very little extra, or go on to San Francisco on an "open jaws" itinerary for about $100 more.

Airlines compete heavily for discretionary travel. Flights in and out of tourist areas are apt to be more heavily discounted than flights catering to business people who have to fly regardless of cost. If you consult the travel section of your Sunday paper or get the Sunday New York Times, you will often find deeply discounted fares to resort areas such as Orlando (Disney World). If you find some bargains such as these to cities near where you will be interviewing, it may pay to book the cheap flight and rent a car. Indeed, sometimes a rental car will be part of the package.

Most business travelers return home for the weekend. To attract the discretionary traveler, airlines often offer deep discounts on trips that extend over a Saturday night. I recently had to fly from Tallahassee, FL to Austin, TX on business. With two state capitals involved, the cost of weekday travel was hideous. By staying over Saturday, I was able to save almost $600.

Regardless of the number of seats sold, transcontinental airlines have to get the planes that flew to the West Coast during the day back to the East Coast by the beginning of the next business day, in spite of the three-hour time zone differential. In order to fill otherwise empty seats, they may offer reduced "night owl" or "red eye" fares.

Those of you who are "night people" may also save in another way. During the day, the airlines' booking agents are very busy. Their calls are monitored, and they are evaluated by how many calls they can handle in an hour. That is why you often get a busy signal when you dial their toll free "800" number. In the early morning hours, however, the 24-hour "800" numbers have very little traffic, and the bored agents can spend much more time working with you. We have obtained some incredible travel bargains, such as a $198 round trip Miami to London fare, during these early morning conversations.

Whether you call at night or during the day, do not assume that the price you are being quoted is definitive, or even correct. Not only do different airlines have different rates subject to different restrictions, but booking agents differ in their knowledge of the system and their willingness to ferret out bargains. Each flight has only a limited number of discounted seats available, and, of course, full fare passengers have first priority for any available seats. Thus the availability of bargain fares varies. You may be told on Monday that a low fare is unavailable, but if you book at a higher rate, don't expect anyone to notify you if there is a cancellation on Wednesday and the lower rate you initially requested becomes available.

Booking agents can make mistakes computing fares. A newspaper recently did a study in which they called agents and general managers at several different airlines inquiring about the cost of certain flights. They reported that the rates quoted differed substantially, not only between carriers, but also between agents computing fares for a particular flight. In short, if you do not like the rate you are being quoted, hang up and try again later. You may get quoted a lower price. If so, take it. Once you have made your reservation, your fare is locked in. (The exception to this is if there is a general fare increase. In that case your fare is protected only if you have already been ticketed.)

It may be possible for your DCT or your support group to negotiate a special group rate for your internship class. One year the sales manager at our primary airline waived certain restrictions for the internship applicants, such as giving the over-Saturday rate even if they did not stay over. The rationale was that this group of students, who would be doing a great deal of travel on limited budgets, would soon experience a marked increase in income, and it was an excellent way for the airline to build customer loyalty.

Getting there is half the hassle

The combination of high holiday volume and poor weather make December and January bad months to travel. Unfortunately, that's when you usually must interview. Do not schedule tight connections in hub cities, and keep your luggage in your possession. Do not wear casual clothes, such as warm-up suits or shorts, while flying, unless you are prepared to interview in that outfit.

Flight delays. A flight is considered "delayed" if it is 15 minutes or more late in departing from the gate or arriving at the destination gate. Mechanical problems and weather are not counted so as to avoid the temptation to fly an unsafe plane. In 1991, DOT data showed that 17.5% of the flights in the U.S., involving an estimated 80 million passengers, were "delayed" (Gavzer, 1992). Every month the FAA publishes a "list of shame" in which it reports those flights that were delayed more than 80% of the time during the previous month. One month USAir Flight 326 from Boston to Washington was late 100% of the time, with the delays averaging 77 minutes. Airports are also evaluated. Among the five worst are La Guardia, Newark, Chicago/O'Hare, Kennedy and San Francisco (Weiner, 1990). If you are traveling on an airline or through an airport with frequent delays, allow extra time for your connections or consider changing your itinerary.

Losing luggage. Although you should plan to carry your luggage on the aircraft, the airline personnel at the gate may require you to check it. This is most apt to happen if your bag cannot fit under the seat, if you have more than two pieces, or if the overhead compartments are full, which is often the case around Christmas. If your bag is checked it may get lost, or items may be stolen from it, whether or not it is locked. Do not pack anything you cannot afford to lose in a bag that may have to be checked. Dress nicely, and carry a small survival kit with essential toiletries and a change of underwear in your briefcase or purse.

Getting "bumped". Airlines often overbook at peak seasons, such as December, and at prime times, such as late afternoon. When more people with reservations show up than the computer predicted, they are in what they refer to as an

145

"oversold condition." More prosaically it means someone is going to get "bumped."

The best way to avoid being bumped is to have your boarding pass and to arrive at the gate early. Select your seats when you buy your tickets and get your boarding passes issued at the time of ticketing. Then check in at the gate early...at least 45 minutes before flight time. It is the folks arriving at the last minute who have not had their boarding passes stamped who are most likely to be bumped.

Before bumping anyone, the agent will make an announcement that the flight is oversold and will ask for volunteers. If your schedule is loose or you are on the return leg, it may be to your advantage to volunteer to be bumped. At the very least they should offer you a free round trip ticket anywhere in the system that is good for a year. (Check the fine print...it may black out certain dates or be "subject to availability," i.e. only good for standby.) The more oversold they are, the more incentives you may be offered. Perhaps they will offer to make the free ticket good any time or, as they get more desperate, offer a free companion ticket or even cash in addition to the ticket. There may be a stampede of volunteers, so decide early.

It can pay to volunteer. One student on his way home volunteered and was given a free unrestricted round trip ticket anywhere in the U.S. and a seat on another carrier's flight departing an hour later. He actually arrived at his destination several hours earlier than the passengers who remained on the original flight since it developed mechanical difficulties and had to turn back.

If you are bumped, voluntarily or otherwise, you are entitled to certain perks. The airline will usually notify people waiting to meet you at your destination, either by telex or by letting you use the phone. If the next flight out is after a normal mealtime, ask for a <u>free meal ticket</u> so you can have lunch or dinner at their expense. Most airlines have clubs or VIP rooms. If you ask, the gate attendant may give you a card allowing you to wait there. If you have to spend the night, you should ask for lodging at a nearby hotel and meal checks for dinner and breakfast.

<u>Canceled flights</u>. Nice clothes, a polite manner, and a frequent traveler card may also help you get better treatment from harassed ticket clerks if your flight is canceled and you have to be rerouted (as occurred to me on three out of four flights one miserable December). Remember to <u>keep on your person a list of the names and phone numbers of the people you are supposed to see so you can notify them when your plane is canceled or delayed</u>. (See the Travel Planner in Appendix Four.) A <u>long distance telephone credit card</u> and a supply of <u>travelers' checks</u> are other helpful travel accessories.

While the airlines are obliged to provide meals and lodging if you are bumped, this may not apply if the flight has to be canceled, especially if the cancellation is due to weather. Under Industry Rule 240, they must get you to your destination, either on an alternate flight or another airline, but there is no guarantee <u>when</u> you will get there. You will be competing with everyone else who was on your flight for a limited number of seats, and if weather has closed the airport, no one will be going anywhere until it reopens. That is why every winter the newspapers feature photos of stranded passengers sleeping on their luggage.

To lessen your chances of being stranded by a canceled flight, give your airline a number where you can be reached the morning of your flight and arrive early. Airlines may know several hours in advance that a flight will have to be canceled. If they have your number and/or you arrive early, they can put you on an earlier flight or on another airline.

If you miss a flight, you may have to switch to another airline which may not accept deeply discounted or complimentary tickets. Or if your airline goes bankrupt, as one seems to do most every year, other carriers may be reluctant to accept any tickets issued by the insolvent airline. Have a credit card with a high enough credit limit or enough travelers' checks to pay for a new ticket if necessary. If you charged your ticket on the bankrupt airline to a major credit card, the charge should be canceled. Otherwise you are just one more creditor (Gavzer, 1992).

Jumping ship. Sometimes a flight's departure is delayed interminably, supposedly to correct mechanical problems. Sometimes this is a subterfuge. An airline that has two partly filled flights, both going to the same city an hour or two apart, may be tempted to get everyone on board the first flight, delay it for an hour or so, then transfer them to the second so they can fly one full flight instead. This only works if they can stall the passengers seated on the first flight by assuring them the difficulty will be corrected momentarily. Other times there may actually be something wrong.

Your first hint of trouble may be a note on the departure board to "see agent." Or you may surrender your ticket, board the aircraft, and find that 10 minutes after scheduled departure time the door is still open and everyone is standing around. Eventually you may be told that they are awaiting a new crew or checking a leak in the framistat.

Try to find out what is going on. Perhaps, looking out the window, you see that the ground crew has disassembled one of the engines and are quizzically scratching their heads as they gaze at the parts scattered over the tarmac. The flight attendants are sitting down and working on their nails. If you are on a tight schedule, consider taking another flight.

Experienced air travelers carry a copy of the Official Airline Guides North American Pocket Flight Guide that is published monthly and is available in major airports. For every destination in North America, it lists every flight on every airline from every city. If you are on the ground in Los Angeles waiting for your flight to O'Hare to depart, consult the Flight Guide. You will see there are about five dozen other flights going from "LAX" to "ORD" every day. The people who grab their luggage and head for the door when a mechanical problem is announced are hurrying to get on one of these other flights. If you get off, try phoning the other airline first to see if they have seats, especially if the gate is several concourses away. (This is when it would pay to have a cellular phone.) If you decide to switch, make sure you get your ticket back from the agent. You will need it to pay for the new flight.

In the event your destination city is socked in by weather or the delay is caused by a "gate hold" at your destination, changing planes won't help. (However, a cellular phone can still come in handy. When a flight that normally serves dinner was held at the gate well past the normal meal time, one ravenous passenger called Domino's and had a large pizza delivered to the plane.)

Gate attendants are human, and, like all of us, they respond better to people who are polite and considerate. They didn't cause the overbooking or break the framistat, so don't take out your frustration by berating them. Be firm, however, and, if the delay is going to ruin the rest of your life, let the agent know. Although you should not get hysterical, a quavering voice and a controlled tear or two may help.

Car rentals

The only practical way for you to get to some internship centers in distant cities will be to fly there and rent a car at the airport. If you choose to do so, you will find that rates and amenities vary tremendously. Like the airlines, the car rental agencies have a glut of customers during the business week and fewer on weekends. They establish their rates to encourage discretionary travelers.

A major credit card is essential when renting a car; without one, you will be required to leave a humongous cash deposit to guarantee you will return the vehicle. The other requirement, of course, is a valid driver's license. Reserve an automobile in advance, and shop for the best deal. If you work for a state agency or university, you may be able to get a government rate. You may assume that firms whose names emphasize their frugality will give you the best rates. That may not be true. Check out the major firms as well. If you ask, your travel agent can usually find the best rate and reserve you a car.

Find the package that is best suited for your needs on this particular trip. In addition to the daily cost, ask whether there is a mileage fee. If you are not driving very far, a lower daily rate with a 100 mile a day allotment may be best; on the other hand if you are going to be logging a lot of miles, a higher daily rate and unlimited mileage may be more economical.

In choosing a car rental agency, consider whether it is located in the airport or in the boondocks. The greater convenience of the airport location may offset any price differential, especially if you are on a tight schedule.

Make sure you ask if there are discounts available. You may qualify for a discount by virtue of belonging to AAA or some other organization, because you flew in on a certain airline, or by virtue of staying in a particular hotel. I was once given an unexpected discount because I was in uniform when I returned the vehicle... a Scoutmaster's uniform! Make sure you take along all your membership cards and don't forget your driver's license. Also bring along any discount or upgrade coupons you have received from your air line flyer's club or AAA. In winter, especially, having a larger car may be very helpful.

Insurance is a major factor in renting a car. Many companies make as much from the insurance as they do from the rental. If you already have auto insurance, check with your carrier. If you are covered while driving a rental car, and almost everyone is, refuse the added coverage. (Remember your AAA probably covers any emergency road service.)

Before you leave, make sure you know the policy on gasoline. Are you expected to bring the car back with the same amount of gas as you found in it, fully fueled or what? How much will they charge you if they have to refill it? If you are not sure how to get to the internship ask for a map and directions, and make sure you know how to get to the place where you must return the car. In fact, if I know I am going to be in a hurry to make my flight on the way back, I check it out before I leave the airport to make sure I know how to find it.

When you pick up the car, look it over for obvious damage. If you see anything, get another car or have it noted on your contract so they do not charge you for it. Similarly, check to make sure you have a spare tire. If you don't, ask that one be provided, or, if you feel daring, make sure the absence of a spare is noted on your contract so you don't get accused of selling it.

Renting and returning a car is much simpler if you have a prearranged rental number. Most companies have a program whereby you fill out an application form that lists your preferences in vehicle, insurance options, driver's license number, preferred mode of payment, discounts you may be eligible for, credit card numbers and so on. They will issue you a card which the clerk puts in a computer and the rental contract emerges printed correctly. When you return the

car, if you are in a hurry, you merely have to
record the mileage, insert the papers in a time
clock, and drop it in a slot. The bill will be
mailed to you.

Lodging: Reducing the "rack rate"

Non-smoking room

The least expensive lodging is, of course,
to stay with a relative or friend. Often a fellow
student from your school who is currently interning at the place where you are interviewing will
put you up. If you hope to visit someone, you
should check well ahead of time, before you have
booked your tickets.

Realistically, unless you have a large extended family or are only applying to places close
to home, you will have to spend some nights in
hotels or motels. If you are driving to internships
or if you rent a car, you will have many more
options than if you are relying on public transportation. This is where the AAA tour books come in
handy, because you can use the spotter maps to
locate hotels in the vicinity and then check the
rates that are listed. Be advised, though, that
the AAA book does not include all the motels in an
area, and the fact that a place is not included
does not necessarily mean that it is unacceptable.

If you look at the hotel maps for most cities, you will see that there are generally three
clusters that have a high density of accommoda-
tions: 1) the "downtown" area, especially in the
proximity of a civic or convention center; 2) the
airport; and 3) near the exits to the Interstate or
"beltway" around the city. Typically the downtown
area is the most expensive, catering to commercial
travelers who use their room to conduct business
and who can put a $100 to $200 room on their
expense account.

Next most expensive is the airport area,
especially the chains such as Hyatt, Marriott, and
Sheraton. However, there are often smaller places,
such as Comfort Inns, that lack such amenities as

a pool or a lounge, that are less expensive, i.e. in the $30 to $40 bracket. These are the motels airlines use for stranded passengers.

Least expensive, typically, are the places near the Interstate exit. They cater to automobile travelers who are looking for a place to sleep and little else; since motorists are, by definition, mobile, they can shop for bargains, and these motels must be economical to compete. If you have wheels, you can often save money by staying at one of these places on the edge of town and driving in to the medical center instead of booking a room across from the hospital. Of course, the cost is even lower if you team up with another applicant to share travel and lodging expenses.

Although everyone knows you can shop for air fares, fewer people are aware that hotel rates are very negotiable, especially at the more expensive places. No matter where you stay, always ask for a lower rate. When you book your room, ask the price. Whatever they quote you, respond, "Oh, that must be your rack rate" and ask what discounts are available. ("Rack rate" is a key phrase and it shows you know the ins and outs of the hotel business.)

You can probably qualify for a discount on the basis of some group to which you belong. APA membership entitles you to special rates at Holiday Inn, Howard Johnson, and Sheraton. AAA membership is worth a 10% discount at participating hotels and motels. If you are a state employee, such as a Teaching Assistant at a state university or a psychology trainee at a state hospital, try asking for the "government" or "state of West Idabama" rate. You may be told to be prepared to show government ID or a letter of authorization on state stationery when you arrive. However, the only place I actually have been asked for my government ID is in the District of Columbia. Again, being well dressed helps at the check-in desk.

If the government rate does not apply, ask for an educational or student discount. See if your AAA, APA, or Airline Frequent Traveler membership entitles you to a discount. You will soon learn which chains cater to which groups. Or your travel agent may be able to book a combination package that includes airfare, hotel and car, all at a discount.

Many major medical centers have negotiated special medical or hospital visitor rates with one or more local hotels and motels. Ask the secretary who books your interview. If the secretary does not know, simply ask for a hospital rate when you make your reservation. As a hospital visitor, Hilton recently charged me only $39 for a $120 room.

Each hotel has only a limited number of discounted rooms, so the earlier you book, the better your chances. The nice thing about hotels, in contrast to airlines, is that you do not have to pay in advance and there is no penalty for canceling your reservation.

Other things are also negotiable. You might be able to get a free breakfast, for example, especially if you belong to the hotel chain's preferred guest program. Other perks can include a room upgrade, a complimentary cocktail, concierge service and a morning newspaper. If you prefer a nonsmoking room or a king size bed, ask for them. If you are a woman traveling alone, mention this and ask for a secure room. Not only will this lessen the likelihood that you will be followed across a parking lot by some polyester-clad creep from the lounge, but it may also get you upgraded to a superior room at the same price.

The time to negotiate discounts and special perks is when you book the room, not at midnight after you have arrived, tired and disheveled, from the airport. It is best to call the hotel or motel directly, rather than the 800 number, if you are trying to get a discount. The person answering the 800 phone may not have the necessary authority. If you cannot get what you want, ask for the Assistant Manager. If they still will not budge, try someplace else. (As a general rule, the better the hotel and the more they are geared to business travelers, the greater the discount you can get.)

Even with all these maneuvers, if the hotel is heavily booked, the best you may be able to do is the "corporate" rate. That gets you a nice room, but it is very expensive. It is best to try somewhere else, but if you must stay at that hotel, take that rate and ask to be put on stand-by for the lower government or educational rate. When you check in, ask the clerk if the lower rate room opened up and you may be pleasantly surprised.

Most airlines have arrangements with major hotel chains, so you get additional frequent traveler miles when you fly in on that airline. Ask for a coupon at the desk, fill it out, and leave it with the clerk.

Whatever the rate you manage to negotiate, make sure you obtain and record a confirmation number or name. No matter what your expected arrival time, it is a good idea to guarantee your room for late arrival by providing a major credit card number. If for some reason you cannot make it, call and cancel before 6:00 PM or you will have to pay for your (unused) room. Make sure you get a cancellation number, and later examine your credit card bill to make sure the charge does not appear.

Like airlines, hotels sometimes overbook, especially when there is a big convention or a major sporting event in town. Also, in many states, guests are not legally required to leave when their reservations expire. If the airports or highways are closed because of bad weather, many guests will stay on and new arrivals are out of luck, even though they have guaranteed reservations. If you arrive after all the rooms at your rate have been occupied, the desk clerk has three choices: 1) check you into a better room at the same rate if one is available; 2) get you reservations at another hotel (and have the van take you there); or 3) shrug and express regrets.

If you were a desk clerk in this situation and you were confronted with: 1) a polite, well-dressed young person who is a member of your "Honored Guest" program, 2) some smelly slob who is clad in shorts and a stained tank top, and 3) an arrogant SOB who is calling you names and pounding the counter, which one would you discretely signal to come back in 20 minutes and then upgrade to the Presidential Suite? (If you want to try overkill, you might mention to the desk clerk how much you admire his or her ability to deal with such contentious people and offer to fetch the poor harassed person a cup of coffee or a soft drink while they work on your problem.)

Even with all these discounts, travel is very expensive. If your parents or relatives inquire about a suitable Christmas gift, you might mention a go-anywhere ticket if they again become available, or they may be able to provide you with some free travel if they have saved up some frequent traveler coupons. If you can cadge a first class upgrade coupon, take it by all means. Luggage and clothing are also quite acceptable. If you have not purchased a new suitcase or garment bag in the last three years, you will be amazed at the advances that have been made.

Dressing for travel and interviews

You may need to add to your wardrobe. You will have to dress professionally when on internship, so you might as well get the clothes now. Assuming you are going to be on the road for several days, I would suggest you take at least two complete outfits, preferably ones you can mix and match. A solid color navy blue business suit and a light or medium gray one in compatible fabrics (preferably 100% wool in a climate-suitable weight) can provide at least four outfits as you swap your jackets with your slacks or skirts. Dark brown and tan provide another compatible combination. Women have a greater range of colors to mix and match, such as red, black, or white. Or consider a solid color suit and sports coat/slacks outfit for men, and suit or blazer/skirt outfit plus a business dress for women. (Stick with solids when you are building your wardrobe. Patterned materials are much less versatile and hence less cost effective.)

Regard your jacket as framing for your blouse and scarf, or shirt and tie. Only one item should be patterned. If you wear a patterned suit or jacket, keep the other items plain. If your jacket and the shirt or blouse are solid, then you can have a patterned tie or scarf. Jewelry should be understated and complementary to the overall outfit. Remember, you want people to focus on you and not be distracted by excessive or clashing accouterments.

Sweaters and slacks/skirts will probably be appropriate when you are working at most internship agencies (although some insist on coat and tie for men and a suit or dress for women), but I feel this is too casual for interviewing. Nevertheless, take along some "nice" but less formal clothes for going out in the evening with the present interns. Be prepared for cold or inclement weather. Now is the time to invest in that tan all-weather coat with the removable lining.

Remember that you will be doing a lot of walking, so take well-shined leather shoes that are attractive but comfortable. This is not the time for five inch stiletto heels (especially for the men), but don't go to the other extreme and wear running shoes or (shudder) sandals. Gender-appropriate hose is a must.

Murphy's Law applies with a vengeance when it comes to traveling. To paraphrase the bumper sticker, "Spills Happen," usually the first day out, so avoid those light colored fabrics that do not blend well with tomato sauce. Familiarity with the operation of a sewing needle and an iron (both of which will be available where you stay) may prove useful. You can minimize difficulties by taking the time to check for loose buttons, wobbly eyeglass frames and frayed shoelaces before you pack.

What to take

Prepare for internship travel as you would for a backpacking trip in the Andes. Include "emergency equipment" such as spare glasses or contacts, a sewing kit (with extra buttons), a styptic pencil, nail clipper, band aids, spare shoelaces, extra pantyhose, and clear nail polish to repair the pantyhose in your travel kit. You may never need them, but if you do you will really need them. "Traveling light" is fashionable, and there is no need to carry excessive amounts of heavy items such as shampoo, but it is important to take everything you might need. This is not the time to conduct an empirical test of whether that new deodorant really does last 72 hours without replenishing. Which is worse, carrying along an extra 4 oz. or asphyxiating the internship selection committee?

Invest in a box of Ziploc freezer bags and, after squeezing the air from bottles of liquids, seal the bottles in bags. (Liquids expand and leak at altitude.) Instead of loading up your luggage with huge and heavy bottles, just take a small container with the minimal necessary amount of each item. If you cannot find 2 oz. travel sizes, buy small plastic bottles at the nearest discount drug store and decant the appropriate amount of whatever therein.

Is this beginning to sound like a Scout Manual? Well, as a matter of fact, I do carry a Swiss Army knife in my permanently-packed travel kit; it has reattached the handle of a briefcase, repaired eyeglasses, sharpened pencils, and opened innumerable soda bottles. A mini-flashlight that stays beside my bed in case of fire, also helps me find my way around a strange motel room in the dark. Don't forget a small travel alarm, and remember to reprogram it as you change time zones.

Interviewing and travel are both stressful, so don't be surprised if your body turns on you. Even if it functions with the regularity and precision of a Swiss chronometer at home, it can go totally out of synch on the road, especially if you have jet lag to contend with. Take along whatever you use to deal with bodily emergencies such as gastrointestinal distress, allergies, headaches, hemmorhages, cramps, etc.

Go to AAA and get maps of where you will be visiting. One year an applicant got hopelessly lost, gave up, and returned home without interviewing. After turning South instead of North more often than I care to remember, I added a small compass to my kit. In addition to helping me orient myself when I leave an airport or a subway, it can be invaluable in finding my way around strange hospital corridors, many of which seem to have been designed with minimal spatial cues to thwart patients bent on leaving.

Before you depart make arrangements for staying in touch with your home base. Other internships may call while you are off interviewing, so your friends and DCT should know how to reach you.

A word about answering machines. These devices can be invaluable, especially those that automatically "time stamp" your messages and from which you can retrieve your calls by phone while you are on travel status. However, do not rely on them. Tapes can get overloaded, especially if you have some "friend" or former lover who feels it is amusing to recite poetry or play music into your machine. Power outages can erase your messages.

Most important, from the time you send in your first application until the week after Notification Day, remember that your future Training Director may be calling. If you have "amusing" or "entertaining" messages on your machine, ask yourself if this is really how you want to impress your top choice TD. Selection staff at internships have told me that one of their greatest frustrations is repeatedly listening to "cute" messages on applicants' answering machines. That aggravation may determine whether or not they call back. (Some students have told me that this advice alone is worth the price of this book.)

Other tips

Six weeks or more before you leave for interviews, get a flu shot. Except for a test tube, which it rather resembles, an airplane is the best place in the world for exchanging air-borne viruses with people from all over the world. The hospitals you may be visiting also have more than their share of germs. If you don't pick up something while traveling, you will from one of your fellow applicants. By Ground Hog Day, many of the intern applicants who didn't get their flu shots will be sick.

CHAPTER EIGHT:

THE SITE VISIT AND INTERVIEW

The personal interview and visit to the internship facility is the most time-consuming and expensive part of the process. A Midwestern DCT estimates his students spend about $2,000 interviewing (Fox, 1991). Students attending less centrally located schools might incur even greater expenses.

Training centers' policies with regard to interviewing are just as uniform as their application forms; that is not at all. A few programs refuse to interview anyone. Others interview by invitation only, and many require interviews in person or by telephone. To add to the confusion, Fox (1991, p. 34) reports, "Some programs apparently use the interview as a screening device by indicating to applicants that interviews are optional, but that willingness to appear for a personal interview will be viewed as an index of strong interest in their program."

Some internships conduct interviews whenever applicants can arrange to visit, some confine interviewing to a two or three week period, and some require everyone to present themselves on a specific date with no exceptions permitted. As Fox (1991, p. 34) remarked, "Some directors are understanding and flexible in responding to the realities of students' life circumstances, others are embarrassingly rigid and callous."

If at all possible, make an effort to go to the training center to see it for yourself and interview in person. Not only should it enhance your candidacy, but it is your single best opportunity to obtain the data you need to evaluate the program and its personnel. As I noted earlier, every year some students change their opinions radically after actually seeing the internship settings and meeting the people. I personally find a site visit indispensable in sizing up a setting.

An exception is when the facility has rigged the situation so that you are deprived of an adequate opportunity to evaluate their program. Recently one of my students traveled 2,000 miles at considerable cost and personal inconvenience to sit in a cafeteria with 50 other applicants on a Saturday morning listening to the TD read the program's brochure to them. After a brief tour of the grounds, they were sent on their way. While he was understandably indignant, he had learned enough about the program to cross it off his list.

In the middle of December, after you have submitted all your applications and before you start traveling, there will be a lull during which you can catch your breath, regroup and get ready for the next phase. This is a good time to prepare for interviewing.

One of the best ways to get ready is to read the advice of previous students who have been through the process and published their accounts. I recommend the articles by Burt (1985), Kingsley (1985), and Jacob (1987). These first person accounts by actual survivors have an authenticity that cannot be duplicated. They will help prepare you for some of the mood swings you will experience and give you the concrete practical advice that can only be provided by someone who has been through the process, such as taking advantage of every opportunity to go to the bathroom because you never know if you will get another chance.

Their accounts are also full of "war stories" about the strange things that can happen and the peculiar people you might encounter. Fox, who was a TD before becoming a DCT, complains about, "... the high-handedness, arrogance, unprofessionalism and plain rudeness which a number of our students encounter each year in their dealings with some of our colleagues in some internship programs" (1991, p. 35). Fox is correct; I have been out there myself and experienced it first hand, so don't think this behavior is reserved for students. Some training personnel are equal-opportunity jerks. Fortunately these turkeys are in the minority, and, as Fox notes (1991, p. 35), "We all have our bozos." Nevertheless, attitudes like this rankle and are an added aggravation at an already difficult time in your lives. So, during your travels, if you think you have wandered into the Twilight Zone, recall these accounts. It may not be reassuring to realize that this is reality, but at least you will know others have survived similar insanity.

Also helpful are articles by Training Directors on how they view the interviewing and internship selection process. I recommend the articles by Belar and Orgel (1980), Grace (1985), and Monti (1985), many of which can be found in the book edited by Dana and May (1987). May, Rice and Birckhead (1990) report that many TDs rely on the interview as their primary selection device. They are as interested in intangible aspects such as rapport, a sense of humor and flexibility, as they are in the actual content. Maintaining eye contact and shaking hands firmly may be as important as what you say.

Hersh and Poey (1984) have provided a convenient and concise outline of questions that TDs may ask you and that you can ask them. They also suggest some questions you should not ask. Appendices Five and Six provide you with questions asked by interviewers and other questions you can ask them. Study this material, assimilate it, and then integrate it into your own personal style. Often it is a good idea to role-play or practice interviewing using a fellow student or your major professor as the interviewer. Then switch and you try taking the TD's role. You will find it greatly increases your understanding of what the person on the other side of the desk is looking for.

Scheduling interviews

As I have noted before, I recommend that you visit all the sites you are considering if it is at all possible. This is for your own benefit. More than once an applicant has walked into a place and immediately sensed, "This is not for me."

Policies on interviewing differ. Whereas some internships will simply not consider any applicant they have not personally interviewed, at least one internship refuses to interview anyone. Because they are located in a remote area, they reason that interviewing would give local applicants an undue advantage because travel to and from the facility is so difficult and expensive. If applicants insist, the Training Center does set aside two Saturdays when candidates can visit the facility and listen to lectures on the various rotations. People who have participated reported that this was not a worthwhile expenditure of time and effort.

Most internships will interview anyone who requests an opportunity, either in person or by phone. Indeed, not interviewing is often seen as a sign of disinterest, and, as we noted in Chapter One, perceived disinterest is deadly to your candidacy. Some internships set aside a couple of specified weekends for interviewing, and others make individual arrangements with each candidate. Some settings first screen the overall pool of applicants and invite only a select subgroup.

Realistically, however, you may not have the time or money to interview everywhere. This is especially true if your top priority is a particular internship experience, such as a children's hospital, since such facilities are scattered all across the country. Do not write off a place because it will not be possible for you to interview

there in person. Our students who have participated in telephone interviews have reported that
they got a good feel for the facility. They have
been accepted at very competitive programs and
had good experiences at these internships. In my
opinion, telephone interviews usually help the site
in selecting students more than they do the
students in evaluating the sites.

You should recognize that the internship
selection process, including interviewing, can
place a great strain on a training center. The
present interns are nearing the end of their first
rotations and being evaluated, and the training
personnel must continue to deal with their regular
clinical duties throughout internship season. After
they have interviewed dozens of bright well qualified applicants, staff can be forgiven for not
being enthusiastic about seeing more. Therefore,
it behooves you to request an interview as soon
as possible. Not only will it help you make more
economical travel arrangements, but latecomers
may simply be told that there are no appointments
left.

Winiarski (1986) notes that you can begin
to get a feel for a place when you first call
requesting an interview. "Does the secretary greet
you warmly, or are you put on hold for 30
minutes? Are you offered lodging with other interns...or are you told, 'See you at the office at
9:30 Monday' and then expected to fend for
yourself?"

If your request for an interview is refused,
check with your DCT. As a student you probably
had to deal with a secretary or executive assistant, but your DCT will have access to the Training Director and can find out directly what the
problem is. It may be that your folder appears
incomplete. If there is a perceived problem with
your application or your apparent credentials,
your DCT can find out. If there is some misper-
ception involved, your DCT may be able to correct
it. It could be that someone simply made a mis-

take. One year a TD told me that his secretary had misinterpreted something he had said and had denied interviews to anyone who called after January 1. Whatever the reason for your refusal, your DCT may be able to arrange an interview for you by dealing directly with the TD.

If not, being denied an interview is not the kiss of death, as discouraging as it may be. On Notification Day one of our students actually received an offer from an internship that had earlier turned down his request for an interview. He enjoyed telling them that he had already accepted a position at a rival training center.

Winiarski (1986) recommends that, if possible, you arrange to visit your lowest ranked choices first. "This will benefit you in two ways. First, if you flub up some early interviews, the damage won't be as great, and you can learn from the experience. Second, you'll have more data going into the more important interviews, and therefore know more about what to look for and have better questions to ask." His advice, of course, assumes that your motivation will remain constant. If you wait too long, you may be burned out and no longer care what sort of an impression you make. Perhaps the best advice is to schedule yourself some rest days so you can recuperate between visits.

When you make an appointment for an interview, make sure you know exactly where you are supposed to report and how to get there. If you are going to be driving, ask about the availability of parking. If possible, find out who you will be talking to so you can learn more about them before you interview.

Preparing for the interview

Before visiting a site, make sure you do your homework. Review the facility's program descriptions and brochure. Nothing discourages training staff more than applicants who ask questions that show they have not done their basic homework and know little or nothing about the program. If you are interested in children, don't ask, "Do you have a child rotation?" If you read the brochure you should know that there is a child rotation. Instead inquire about what sorts of training experiences are available on the child rotation or how interns get chosen.

The Directory of the American Psychological Association (APA, 1989) is a useful tool in learning more about the internship personnel. Usually the brochure will list the key faculty members, but if not, the Directory's geographical index will provide the names of those people who listed the training center as their address. By looking up the names of the training personnel, you can learn where they got their degrees, their credentials, where they have previously been employed and their interests as reflected in the divisions to which they belong. Your reference librarian can guide you to other   directories such as the Who's Who series, but the APA Directory should suffice.

Using 3 X 5 inch cards, that you can quickly review before an interview, make notes on salient aspects of their careers. If you are familiar with where they did their graduate work and interned, you may be able to identify some mutual acquaintances. Perhaps they know some other students who graduated from your university or they might know someone on your faculty.

As you know, the Psychological Abstracts has an author index. Take the time to look up the people you will be meeting, identify some of their writings, and obtain them from the library. Not only will this help you evaluate the setting and the caliber of personnel, but you can impress the interviewer with your knowledge of his or her research. This is also a time to recall those papers written by internship personnel that you observed at professional meetings or workshops. You don't have to be profound. Just say, "I was interested in the work you did with Fistula on peptic ulcers; have you done anything further in that area?" (Of course, be prepared to respond when you are asked, "What aspect of that study interested you?")

Going to the interview

When you travel to the internship, make sure you take along all the materials you will need. Take copies of all your   notes, lists of specific questions to ask at each internship, and the internship's brochures so you can review them before starting your round of appointments. Also take a duplicate copy of your completed application forms in case a part of your application has been lost (they will say never received).   Don't forget your Travel Planner and the 3 X 5 cards on the people you will probably be meeting. If you have business cards with your name and phone number(s) on them bring them along, too.

Always take extra copies of your resume. The internship may not be sufficiently well organized or have the resources to provide every person you see with a copy of your CV, and it is not realistic to expect that everyone has taken the time to review all the CVs in the central file cabinet, especially if it is one of those "interview everybody" weekends. So bring along extra copies to give to the interviewers.

Allow plenty of time to get to your first appointment. Indeed, if you get in the night before, I recommend you do a reconnaissance trip and locate exactly where it is you will be going the next morning. Count on getting lost. When I visit internships, I always have one of our present interns drive me in from the airport and half the time they get lost, even though they have lived there several months. Even if you do not get lost, parking is usually a terrible hassle at any major medical center. This may be a good time to spend a few extra dollars on a taxi; while the cab drivers usually manage to get lost too, at least you don't have to worry about the parking.

One advantage of visiting each internship is that you can observe how they deal with you and the other applicants. Some places will be very well organized. You will be given a schedule of appointments, you may be escorted around by one of the present interns, arrangements will be made to provide you with lunch, and, as you go from office to office, you will note that the people you meet have copies of your CV and have taken the time to read it. At other places, none of these nice things will happen. You may be one of a herd of applicants that is lectured to and then marched from place to place on a cursory tour. The people you meet may be harassed and act like seeing you is just one more annoyance in another difficult day. These observations tell you a lot about a setting and its attitude toward students.

After a while, as you travel from place to place, your perceptions of the various sites will begin to blur. After visiting a site, take 20 minutes to write down your impressions while they are fresh. (Later share them with your support group.) _tape record_

Questions you may be asked

The interview process is a time for mutual evaluation. You will be evaluating the personnel and the setting, and they will be evaluating you. This means everyone, including the current interns who may be showing you around or taking you out for pizza. They will probably be asked for their impressions shortly after you leave for your next visit.

Be prepared to answer why you feel this internship would be good for you. This is a natural question, and does not infringe on any APPIC rules. Instead it provides you with an opportunity to sell yourself to the staff by focusing on your particular abilities. Use this opportu-

169

nity to comment on your expectations so that you can validate them. One student applied to a facility because of its superb inpatient child/adolescent unit; when the applicant mentioned this, she was told that it had been closed the year before. As disconcerting as this was, it would have been a lot worse to find out after accepting an offer.

You will no doubt be asked why you are applying to this particular facility. Be reasonably frank. That is, do not say, "My DCT insisted I apply to one really fourth rate place so that I can be sure of getting an offer somewhere." Instead focus on programmatic elements and particular personnel with whom you would like to work. This is a good opportunity to mention any favorable comments made by previous interns from your school. It not only helps to remind the person that your predecessors have done well there, but finding a mutual acquaintance is often a major turning point in an interview.

You can also comment knowledgeably on the research being done by the training staff. Having previously located and read their publications, you can discuss their work with insight (and admiration). This will convince them that you are a very intelligent and discerning individual.

After reciting all the professional reasons, do not be afraid to mention other, nonprofessional, reasons why you are applying, such as climate or geography. The fact that you want to be near aged or infirm parents, or that you hope to locate in the area, are perfectly valid considerations. They should not be the only factors, but Training Directors listen for such comments since they suggest you are likely to accept an offer if it is made.

As Hersh and Poey (1984) point out in their article, you may well be asked detailed questions regarding your professional experience, theoretical orientation and so forth. You may be asked to conceptualize a current case or to describe the populations with which you have worked. If so, don't get annoyed because all of this information is in that resume you so carefully constructed. The interviewer simply wants to hear a sample of your professional verbiage. Can you discuss a case coherently, or describe and give the rationale for a therapeutic intervention? Underneath, the interviewer is asking, "If I send this person on a consult to Ward 22, will our service be embarrassed?" So use this as another opportunity to impress the interviewer with your ability to think clearly under stress and to formulate cogent responses. Give them a sample of what they can expect from you in a case conference if you attend that facility.

Remember, you are applying to a <u>training</u> facility, so they should not expect you to be a fully qualified professional. <u>Be honest about your experience, indicating what your areas of competence are and where you need additional training.</u> Remember your self-analysis and the reasons why you applied to this particular internship.

During your site visit be prepared to back up the claims you made in your application. One year I mentioned in my letter of recommendation that a non-Hispanic applicant was fluent in Spanish. Sure enough, one interview was conducted entirely in Spanish.

You may be asked some questions that stump you. <u>If so, it is better to confess to your ignorance of that topic than to try to fake expertise.</u> Winiarski (1986) recalled that he had mentioned having a course that dealt in part with multiple personality disorders. When the interviewer asked him if he was familiar with that literature, he gulped and replied, "No, not really, just what I heard in class." The interviewer then presented Winiarski with a comprehensive review of the literature on the subject he had just published. Winiarski (1986) noted, "My interview would have been over immediately if I had pretended knowledge I didn't have."

One of the disadvantages about applying for a psychology internship is that you spend a lot of time talking with psychologists. Some of them feel compelled to act "psychological," and approach the interview with a diagnostic mind set. So don't be dismayed if some ask questions about matters such as your family life. One applicant was asked to report the most negative thing she could think of about her father; when she stated she thought he was a fine man who had put all of his children through college under very difficult circumstances, she was accused of resisting.

Another student was interviewed by six psychiatrists who sat in a circle taking verbatim notes. She was quizzed about everything except her masturbation fantasies and they seemed likely to start on that topic when time ran out. You do not have to answer such questions. If interviewers begin getting that personal, you can ask them why they think this information is relevant, or simply declare that it is none of their business. Remember that in normal employment interviews, the interviewer is not even supposed to ask your marital status, much less pry into your personal life.

Once in a while, perhaps out of boredom, someone might toss in an off-the-wall question to see how you react to the unexpected. One interviewer liked to ask candidates what it was they hoped he would not find out about them. (If someone tries this, tell them you hope they won't discover that you are a workaholic.) The nastiest question I have ever heard of was in an interview jointly conducted by several psychiatrists, one of whom asked the applicant to tell a joke. The candidate thought a moment and responded with a story about a young woman who discovered she was pregnant shortly after her boyfriend, who was a psychiatrist, had jilted her. She chose to have the child without telling him. When the psychiatrist eventually found out, he told her that he would have married her had he known. She replied that she was aware of that, but she and her parents had decided that having one bastard in the family was enough. After a pause, during which no one laughed, the interviewer commented, "That was a very hostile story." The candidate replied, "That was a very hostile question."

I doubt if anything this bad will happen to you, but if something of this nature does occur, maintain your equanimity. Deal with the question or request as best you can, asking for clarification if necessary, and simply note that this place, too, has its share of bastards.

Asking questions of the interviewer

Each person you talk to wants to get to know you. Most will ask if you have any questions. This is their way to be helpful and to learn more about you. Nothing is tougher on the interviewer than the person who simply says, "No." As one Training Director remarked with exasperation, "It is inconceivable that a person seriously planning to spend a year of his or her life here has no questions."

Even if it has been a long day, when the fifth interviewer asks you if you have any questions, don't reply, "No, the others already answered them all." If you do this, you will spend the rest of the time staring at each other. Recall some questions from Appendix Six, or ask where the interviewer interned. Presumably it was either at the same place, or somewhere else. If the interviewer actually interned there, you can ask how often interns take positions on staff and launch into all the questions you normally ask current interns, as well as for comments on how life changes once you obtain your degree. If the person interned somewhere else, you can always ask how this internship compares with the place the interviewer attended. Such a comparative approach often provides new perspectives and you can be sure the answers will not be ones you have already heard. The point is not to shut off the dialogue. Ask questions that require elaboration

rather than a simple "yes" or "no." <u>Remember you</u>
<u>are being evaluated in part on the basis of your</u>
<u>interviewing skills.</u>

Your interviews will probably be with a variety of people: staff, present interns, and the Training Director. Use your interviews with different people to cross check information and get data on different aspects of the program, i.e., clientele, working conditions, the relation of psychology to psychiatry (always important at medical centers), number and nature of colloquia, etc. How does the staff's perception of how rotations are assigned or the balance between training and service agree with the students'? What is it the staff seeks in an intern?

The only thing worse than asking no questions is to ask a really stupid question. For most Training Directors, one of the stupidest questions you can ask is for a "general description" of the program. This tells the interviewer that you did not read the brochure they went to such pains to produce. As one Training Director said, "A student must be pretty dumb to come all the way here to apply for an internship when he doesn't know anything about the program."

Prepare <u>specific</u> questions in advance. As in any job interview, the interviewer will be more impressed by inquiries relating to professional matters such as the nature and extent of supervision than with questions about the number of days off, coffee breaks, etc. How you phrase a question can be important. The interviewer will be more impressed with your eagerness to learn if you ask how many seminars are <u>offered</u> as opposed to how many are <u>required</u>. If you think certain training experiences are important, this is the time to determine whether they will be available.

Don't be afraid to ask about general living conditions in the area. Rather than being considered "unprofessional," it tells the TD that you are seriously considering what is involved in moving to this locality. One of our recent applicants was a single mother with a 10 year old child. She was very concerned about such things as school districts, day care facilities, drug use in the schools and so forth. One TD she grilled on these subjects later called to tell me how impressed he was with this woman's professional maturity, sincerity and commitment to being a good parent. He made her an offer and was truly disappointed when she chose to go to another city that she felt would be better for her son.

Dealing with beverages

A word about coffee and other beverages. When you are touring internships, you will soon find that offering a visitor coffee or a beverage is a part of the etiquette. Don't accept.

Whatever the beverage, it is rarely available in the interviewer's office. If you accept, the interviewer is obliged to go down to wherever the beverage area is, locate a reasonably sterile receptacle, and mix the beverage from whatever ingredients are at hand. The only thing you can be sure of is that it will not be the way you prefer it.

Often the coffee center is in the secretarial pool and there will be a sign indicating that coffee is $ .25. You fumble for change, the interviewer assures you that it is not necessary, and the secretaries glare at you. Then you return to the office with 15 minutes of your allotted 30 dissipated.

So there you sit, with your cup of coffee in one hand, your portfolio for collecting handouts and reprints under one arm, and your notepad in another hand. As you reach for your pen you suddenly realize you have one hand less than you need. So you must, gracefully of course, park something somewhere, while attending to the interviewer's every word and formulating cogent answers.

What is the fate of the beverage? Well, you can always spill it. If you do, it is a toss up whether it is better to spill it on the interviewer's desk or on yourself. (See "Packing for travel.") Or, you can hold it clutched in one hand until the interview is over.

The question then arises what to do with the cup. Do you leave it behind for the interviewer to clean up? Do you take it with you? (Hint: if ceramic cup, leave it; if styrofoam, take it.) You then have to cope with shaking hands with the next interviewer while holding your portfolio, clipboard, pen and coffee cup. However, you do have a ready answer to the next interviewer's question of whether you would like a cup of coffee.

Of course, it is possible that you might actually manage to consume the beverage during the interview. If so, you will proceed to the next interview wondering how to deal with a) an empty coffee cup, and b) a full bladder. In short, unless you are being asked to join a group in the coffee shop, for which refusing would be antisocial, skip the coffee.

Charming the executive assistant

By this point in your training you must have learned that every office has a key person who gets things done. Usually a woman, she may have a title ranging from "executive assistant" to "secretary," but she usually has an office next to the titular head who is called the "Chair" or the "Director." The latter person may think he or she is in charge, but nothing much gets done without the executive assistant's input.

Much of the work of internship selection is the responsibility of the executive assistant. This is the person who makes sure that your application and supporting materials are filed correctly, and that the training staff gets their ratings made. It is she who will probably answer your phone calls requesting information or making appointments.

If possible, meet this person and charm her socks off during your visit. Whatever you do don't alienate her (the surest way to do so is by being patronizing). A friendly executive assistant can be incredibly helpful, especially as Notification Day approaches, and a hostile one can misplace your folder so it never sees the light of day.

Evaluating the setting

While visiting, take the opportunity to get a feel for the atmosphere of the facility: the degree of structure, friendliness, caring for the intern's experience, attitude toward clients and all those other intangibles. Is it fast paced or laid back? Is morale high or do people seem disgruntled and harassed? How do the offices and the patients' areas look to you? How do they smell? Will you be treated as a colleague or a serf? Try to talk to the present interns, but remember they are probably rating you too. If you do not get a chance to talk to them, ask for their home phone numbers so you can call them later.

If possible, check out the town. What would it be like to live there? Get a newspaper and see what the rents are like. Drive through the areas where interns typically live. Will you need to invest in a bulletproof vest if you go for a walk? In short, before you leave, make sure that you have enough information to evaluate each setting on those factors that are most important to you. Also, if others are coming with you, check out the aspects important to them.

At some point review Chapter Two, in which I discussed the aspects of the internship to consider in deciding on priorities, especially those dealing with morale, interdisciplinary relations, collegiality, quality and quantity of supervision and the like. At that time you constructed what amounts to a template of your ideal internship. How well does this internship match that template?

On honesty in communication

At the 1988 APA Convention, we had a panel discussion on interviewing for internships. Everybody, Training Directors, university directors and, especially, graduate students who had been through the process, agreed that the three most important things to remember in interviewing are HONESTY, HONESTY, and HONESTY. This applies to all parties: students, the internship staff, and the university faculties.

The next year, however, at the 1989 APPIC meeting, a few Training Directors stated that they expect all students to lie. The next day, in an APA symposium on ethics in interviewing, of all things, a Training Director actually advised students to lie when asked their choices. When it was my turn to speak, I took strong exception to this view. After the meeting a number of TDs stated they had been appalled at his advice.

In the first edition of this book, published in 1990, I wrote, "If these events are any indication, the level of trust among students, TDs and DCTs appears to be declining." This appears to have changed for the better. At that time there was no specific rule that prohibited internship staff members from asking you to rank your choices. (There had been such a rule previously, but somehow it had been inadvertently deleted when the APPIC members voted on Early Acceptance vs. Uniform Notification.) This oversight has been corrected. In a special "Intern Selection Advisory," the APPIC Executive Committee notified its members, "...that it is not acceptable to ask interns their ranking before Notification Day" (Douce, 1990, p. 59), and this principal is now encoded in rule 3-C of the APPIC Guidelines. (See Appendix One.)

During the interviewing process, you are shielded by this rule. There is no reason in the world why you should be expected or required to indicate anything more than sincere interest during the interviewing phase. How can you rank settings until you have seen them all? The people you are visiting would certainly feel you had abused their hospitality if you came to an interview having already made a commitment at a previous site. By the same token, it is unfair to everyone on your list to rank the agencies until you have seem them all. So, be noncommittal. Even if you are enthusiastic about a setting, don't indicate that it is your first choice until after the interviewing phase. Notification Day is several weeks away, and there is plenty of time for communication before then. (We will discuss how to handle requests for information after the interview phase in the next chapter.)

During the close out interview, especially if it is with a member of the selection committee, you may ask how well they feel you fit their needs. Be prepared to respond with your perception of the goodness of fit. Be honest and use this as an opportunity to reiterate the message you want to get across; for example, you might say you think you would fit in because of these reasons, you were impressed with these aspects of the program, the people were real nice and, if you could be sure you would get the child rotation, it would rank high on your list. However do not say anything that can be construed as a commitment. At the other end of the spectrum, don't write a place off prematurely. Keep an open mind and make your decisions after you have surveyed all the options and returned home.

Finally, remember that everyone you meet will be evaluating you, just as you are evaluating them. Some may try to "break your cover." Beware of the intern who, taking you to the airport after your last appointment, casually asks how it went and whether you think you will come if accepted. It is likely that your response will be reported to the Training Director. Be honest, but not naive or ingenuous.

Following up. Your mother no doubt taught you to write "bread and butter" notes after visiting friends to thank them for their hospitality. After you return from interviewing, you should send such notes to all the places where you interviewed. After the interviewing season is over, a major problem for Training Directors is how to determine which interviewees are still interested. A friendly, albeit noncommittal, note, thanking them for their hospitality and repeating that you were impressed with the program, is a good way to communicate the fact that you are still considering their program. If you have some remaining questions, you can use this opportunity to ask. This will put you in a good position to begin the "Endgame."

CHAPTER NINE:

THE END GAME

When you first return from interviewing, you will probably feel relaxed and confident. You got through it and you survived! You held your own in professional interactions with top psychologists away from your home base. It is a heady experience, and you will probably be eager to swap war stories with fellow applicants. Enjoy this feeling while it lasts, because you will soon be entering the most difficult and stress filled stage of the internship selection process, the phase I call the "Endgame."

The Endgame is the culmination of the whole interminable process that began back in the Fall. It is during this period that the training centers finally decide on their selections and the applicants rank their choices. In previous chapters, such as Chapter One on the politics of intern selection, we described some of the concerns the different players have at this stage of the game. In this chapter, we will review some of this material as we describe this final phase in detail. Things are going to get rather tricky before long, and it will help to have all this material available in one chapter, even if some aspects have been mentioned before.

When you applied for college and, later, for graduate school, you filled out your applications, went for your interviews and then waited for the results. Eventually you learned where you had been accepted and made your choice. The final stages of the internship selection process are quite different; be prepared to be an active participant instead of passively awaiting the outcome.

As Notification Day approaches there is usually considerable jockeying for position, negotiating and second guessing. The internships do their best to ensure that their favorite applicants rank them highly, the applicants do their utmost to promote their candidacies at their top choice programs, and the DCTs are busy acting as mediators, facilitators, referees and therapists. The only people who enjoy the Endgame are investors who own stock in the telephone companies.

More politics and poker

By now you have experienced some of the political aspects of the intern marketplace you read about in Chapter One. You know first hand how interested TDs and their staffs are in how you rank their internships...in getting a glimpse of your hole card, to use Chapter One's poker game metaphor. Continuing this analogy, at this stage of the game, the cards have all been dealt, some players have dropped out, and those remaining have finished the first round of betting. Now it is time for you to examine your hand and see if it can be improved.

Discarding and drawing. Once you have reflected on the internships you visited and discussed your reactions with friends, relatives and advisors, review your list. Are there any internships that you would definitely not attend, no matter what? If so, discard them. When they call, do not encourage them; in fact you may advise them not to consider you as an active candidate, especially if a fellow student is very interested in that placement.

Discarding internships you have no interest in attending is to everyone's advantage. It saves the internship staff the trouble of having to decide how to rank your application and leaves them free to pursue more promising candidates. Your frankness can create good will that may later help you professionally. Perhaps you do not want to work in that particular setting, but people move around, and it always helps to have a network of professional contacts who think well of you.

Once you have discarded any internships that you would not attend under any circumstances, reexamine your hand. If your list has gotten too short, and you are doubtful about your chances for acceptance at the remaining institutions, you may want to draw some more cards by submitting another application or two to those centers with late due dates on your "lifeboat list." At this stage of the game, the thought of filling out more applications and going on more interviews will probably be very aversive, but, if your list is truly too short, it is better to do it now than through the Clearinghouse after Notification Day.

Ranking your selections. In late January, ready or not, the actual selection process begins. It is time to rank your choices, and the sooner you do so the better. Using the lists of priorities you established back before your reconnaissance, match your template of what you wanted in an internship with your perception of what each program offers.

In the process of establishing your final rankings, you should consult with other people. These include your DCT and other faculty advisors who may have additional information about certain programs, your fellow applicants, and family members and friends who may be involved in your decision.

Fellow students are another source of information. In our program, we not only have students rank their choices by late January, but we also share our rankings and our impressions of various places with one another. We sometimes find that the story given to some people may differ from what others were told.

Our students cooperate with one another to maximize the chances of our entire group. In their final rankings, they take each others' preferences into account. If we have two or more people first-choicing the same place, I call the TD to determine whether or not they will accept more than one student from a given school. If not, both candidates will need to have more backup. If several students are applying to the same facility, and one or more ranks that internship very high, the rest, who rank it lower should not count on it as a backup or safety net. The internship will typically favor the candidates who rank it high because they are most likely to accept. How do they know? They ask the DCT.

You may discover you need more information. Maybe one of your classmates heard a rumor of a key program change at a certain site. Perhaps your ranking of another depends on your chances of getting a particular rotation, or working with a specific individual. Now is the time to check these details. Call the TD and ask. This also serves to communicate to the TD your continuing interest, and provides the program with some indication of what your concerns are.

You must keep your DCT informed about your rankings, especially if your choices change. Internship staff often call the DCT to discuss students and, if possible, to get an idea of how the students regard their program. If your DCT knows what you want, then he or she can do a great deal to help you get your first choice internship. But if your DCT is uninformed or, worse, misinformed, he or she cannot help your candidacy, and may, inadvertently, damage it.

An example will illustrate this point and also what takes place as Notification Day approaches. "Ginger Curry" had great difficulty making up her mind because her partner could not decide what city would be best for him or, indeed, if he wanted to go along at all. I did not know this, however, and, when Ginger turned in her "final" ranked list of choices, I had no idea that they were actually changing from day to day according to her partner's moods.

Ginger and two other students, "Herb Dill" and "Basil Oregano," had applied to the "Caraway Consortium." Ginger and Herb had both ranked it first, but it was Basil's fifth choice. The TD at Caraway, "Dr. Rosemary Sage," was a good friend and graduate of our program who had accepted several FSU students in previous years.

In late January, Dr. Sage called me to discuss our applicants, as TDs often do when two or more students have applied to the same program. She first asked about Basil. Since he had ranked Caraway fifth and was well regarded by his first choice, I told Rosemary that she had a better chance of recruiting Ginger or Herb. Ginger fit their needs better than Herb, but both had made a good impression, she said. After the Selection Committee met, Rosemary called, indicating that Ginger would be on the first list and Herb on the alternate. Since both had ranked Caraway number one, I said either would accept. (This was before APPIC revised their rules, but informal communications between university and internship staff still occur.)

The Friday before Notification Day, Ginger's partner announced he would go along only if she attended an internship in the Pacific Northwest where he could fish for salmon; the only salmon near Caraway were in cans, so Ginger came in with a new list. At this stage, if Ginger turned down an offer from Caraway, it could strain our relationship with Caraway and damage Dr. Sage's credibility at her program. I told Ginger to call Dr. Sage and indicate she was having second thoughts. Dr. Sage had to be called out of the final Selection Committee meeting, but Ginger was able to get the information to her in time. While disappointed over Ginger's ambivalence, Rosemary said she was very impressed with her honesty.

Over the weekend, Ginger realized she really wanted to go to Caraway, with or without the salmon fisherman, but figured she had irretrievably blown her chance. However, on Notification Day, Caraway made offers both to her and to Herb Dill, and they both accepted. After completing her internship, <u>Dr.</u> Curry stayed on at Caraway, where she became the chief assistant to Dr. Sage, who had been promoted to Chief Psychologist.

You can see why it is important to settle your relationship and other issues before the last week of January, to make a list and stick to it, and to keep your DCT fully informed. Even though this incident eventually worked out, it could easily have ruined the credibility of our program at an important training center, and it caused me and Dr. Sage a lot of needless aggravation at a time when we both had a lot of other things to worry about. (You might say that it served us right; if we hadn't been engaging in these extracurricular discussions, we would not have gotten into this situation. True, but in that event, Caraway would have unsuccessfully attempted to recruit Basil Oregano, rather than considering the candidacies of Ginger Curry and Herb Dill.)

This incident also underscores the fact that in your interviews and conversations with training centers, you are taking the first steps in establishing your professional career. Unethical, inconsiderate or simply impolite behavior can come back to "haunt you in strange ways," while courtesy and consideration can yield long-term benefits. Even if you do not plan to attend a particular program, you are making high level professional contacts, and your attitudes and behavior will be remembered. If you make a good impression it may assist getting a job, if not at that facility then by a referral, as one colleague calls another to ask impressions of this person or that. TDs are the gatekeepers to more than just predoctoral internships, and, in the years to come, their opinions and recommendations can influence whether or not you get invited to a limited access workshop, asked to referee a paper, or nominated for office in a professional society.

The End Game from the Training Directors' perspective. While you are sorting out your cards and deciding how to play your hand, the Training Directors and Selection Committees are doing likewise, albeit on a larger scale. Their decision process is complicated by the fact that they must often consult with consortiums and committees, and consider local policies and politics in formulating their lists, satisfying as many colleagues as possible. As in Maslow's hierarchy, concern for basic survival takes priority over fulfillment of higher order needs. So, the TDs' first goal is to eliminate any candidates they feel are unqualified or unsuitable for various reasons. At this stage they are more concerned with blatant psychopathology, incompetence, and shabby ethics than they are with the niceties of Rorschach interpretation.

Given a pool of acceptable applicants, they want to:

1. obtain the best possible intern class, according to whatever criteria they deem most important, and

2. avoid "being burned" by not filling all their positions. This results from making offers to applicants who hold their positions until all the alternate candidates have made other arrangements, and who then decline the offer.

Most Training Directors believe that the first hours of Notification Day are critical. Obviously, they would like to get an immediate acceptance from each candidate. Failing that, however, it is far better to get an immediate rejection from someone who ranks their program last than it is to receive "holds" from candidates who rank their programs second or third. The TDs know students typically apply to a dozen or more places each, and that some accept the first good offer they receive. Their alternate list can be melting away while their offers are being held by applicants who may eventually decline. That is why many Training Directors seem obsessed with ascertaining how their applicants rank their facilities. Strategic considerations may strongly influence who they select. They may decide not to make an offer to a "superstar" who seems likely to go elsewhere, and call only those applicants that they are reasonably sure will accept. They will be more likely to risk making an offer to a candidate who may not accept if they can be sure that applicant will decide promptly and not hold the offer interminably.

Countdown to Notification Day

After Early Notification and Computerized Matching were voted down, APPIC drafted a more detailed and stringent set of rules governing the Uniform Notification. A copy of this "May, 1991" revision is included in Appendix One of this book, and you should review these rules as Notification Day approaches. Each year the current rules are reprinted in the APPIC Directory and included in each internship's packet of materials. Check these sources to determine if there have been any changes in the rules or in the time Notification Day begins or ends.

The courtship. During January and early February, the internships' selection staffs pore over their lists, looking not only for the most talented students who best fit the needs of their programs, but also for those who are most likely to accept their offers. The interviews were like a flirtation or casual dating; this phase is like a serious courtship, a courtship in which you must keep several suitors interested while you induce your favorite to propose.

Soon, you can expect internships to start calling you. In January, this may be to "answer any questions" and to determine whether you are still interested, but as Notification Day approaches, the courtship gets more serious. Even though they are supposed to wait until Notification Day to "pop the question," what they really want to know is if you will accept a proposal. While you are coping with the TDs who are calling you, be advised that some TDs feel it is inappropriate for them to call applicants. They may be waiting for you to call them, and, if they do not hear from you, they may assume you are not interested. If a program does not call, do not assume that you are out of the running. Give them a call to find out.

Continuing the courtship analogy, just as a would-be fiancee does not have to say "I do" until receiving a proposal of marriage, you do not have to agree in advance to accept an offer from an internship. However, you may fear that without some encouragement, a suitor will never propose. At the same time, you do not want to get a reputation of having promised yourself to everyone in town. This is a confusing time.

Although the rules now prohibit the internships from asking applicants how they rank the programs before Notification Day, there is no rule that forbids applicants from voluntarily informing programs that they are ranked first. So you may get calls designed to give you the opportunity to express your enthusiasm. Consider the following scenario: "Tom Cod," an intern applicant, gets a call from a "Dr. Almondine Dover-Sole," the Training Director at "Halibut Hospital." She asks how Tom is, and whether there is anything about Halibut's program he needs to know. Then Dr. Dover-Sole says, "We are going into a meeting now to decide on our first choices, and I just want to tell you that we are really impressed with your application and we really think you would fit in well here." After a long pause for Mr. Cod to respond, Dr. Dover-Sole might push it one step farther and say, "We certainly hope you like us as much as we like you." As in a courtship, when one party is so bold as to say, "I love you," or even to ask, "Do you love me?", any response other than "Yes," may be interpreted to mean "No."

How does this square with the rules? First, you must realize that APPIC is, at best, a loose confederation, and a few members don't worry about the rules. Rules or no rules, they may flat out ask you how you rank them. Few students dare to file formal charges before Notification Day, and few care to afterwards, especially if they are going to be attending the offending institution. If they do, the internship's defense is that the student obviously misunderstood what was said. If the student should pursue the case and prevail, what would happen? The APPIC Sanctions Committee would probably write a letter criticising their behavior and asking that it not happen again. This is why the most effective action is for the student to notify the DCT of possible violations. The DCT can then sort things out with the TD as provided in APPIC Rule 13.

In our hypothetical example of Dr. Dover-Sole telling Tom Cod how highly he is regarded at Halibut Hospital, she is still acting within the letter of the 1991 rules. What should you do if this happens to you? If you have not decided where you want to go yet, I would say so, especially if you still have some places left to visit. As Notification Day approaches, however, your indecision will have an increasingly negative impact on your candidacy.

Once you have made your rankings, your response will vary depending on how you regard the internship. You obviously want to reassure your first choice, and, if they encourage you to do so and your DCT concurs, you may want to send them a commitment letter as described below.

Facilities that rank closely behind your first choice should be told that you regard them highly, but avoid making a commitment. Your response to these second ranked programs will vary, depending on what sort of feedback you are getting from your first choice. The more remote the likelihood of you getting a bid from your first choice, the more you want to cultivate these facilities.

Obviously, the more information you or your DCT can get about how you stand at your top choices, the better you can play your hand. The rules forbid training centers from disclosing your rank, but your DCT can usually find out if you are clearly out of the running, even if you have not received an exclusion letter. Otherwise the amount of feedback given varies tremendously, especially since the revised rules were adopted. Some programs indicate that certain applicants can expect offers; one, for example, said to a candidate, "I cannot tell you how you stand, but tell your husband to start looking for a job here starting next September." At the other extreme, another was so rigid that it would not even acknowledge it had received an application form from a candidate.

Some programs adopt what is referred to as a "2X," strategy. That is, they try to come up with a list of viable candidates that is twice the number of slots they hope to fill. If they have six slots, they try to identify 12 strong candidates. You or your DCT may be able to find out if you have made the "2X" list. Of course no one is satisfied with this information; everyone wants to know if they are in the top six or bottom six. Some centers are more cautious; one recently used a "5X" strategy, telling 30 candidates they were in the running for six slots.

With your lowest ranked programs, you should be more distant; again, if you would not attend under any circumstances, withdraw your application. If you would attend, but they rank low, don't burn your bridges, especially if you are not getting good feedback elsewhere. Be a bit more circumstantial, take longer to return their calls. In short, do the things you do to discourage a suitor when you don't want to get serious but you do want to stay on good terms. You will be saying, in essence, that you are placing them on your alternate list.

Your DCT can often aid the courting process by acting as a marriage broker. Whereas the rules may constrain the applicant and the TD from discussing the situation forthrightly, the DCT can talk straight to both parties; more important, perhaps, the parties can talk to the DCT when they feel they cannot talk frankly or fully to each other.

The final week. As Notification Day approaches, the pace speeds up. Selection Committees are making their final choices and deciding which candidates to call first. TDs will be calling you and your DCT. Some last minute bargaining may go on...for example, you may be asked how important a given rotation or track is for you. This is particularly apt to occur in facilities which have track-specific selections. If the strongest candidates are all seeking a certain slot and another rotation has few applicants, they may try to see whether some candidates are willing to change.

It is essential at this stage that you stay in touch with your DCT and with your fellow applicants. You must also remain accessible for Training Directors who might call you. One of the major frustrations of internship Training Directors is that graduate students are hard to find, especially during the daytime. Make sure the Directors of the places you are most interested in know how to reach you. Answering machines and fax receivers can be very helpful. Again, make sure you have erased any "cute" messages, ribald songs and so forth from your machine and replaced them with something more appropriate and businesslike.

Notice of exclusion. According to APPIC Rule 2, "Internship program directors must inform applicants who are excluded from consideration as early as possible in the process, and no later than one week before selection day." The big programs that receive 100 or more applications for 10 positions or so, can easily afford to notify 50% or 60% of their applicants that they are out of the running. Less popular programs may be reluctant to exclude many. If they could be certain that all their top ranked applicants would accept, then they could afford to advise the rest to seek other positions. Lacking this knowledge, they will probably not want to exclude, or even discourage, lower ranked applicants because they may need these people on their alternate lists. Such fears may lead some training centers to "string along" applicants who do not have a realistic chance of being accepted. Stedman (1989) reported that one well-regarded program informed numerous applicants that each was "first alternate."

The fact that you have not received an exclusion notice does not necessarily mean that you are a strong contender. If you are really interested in a position, especially if it is your first choice, you should be in touch with that training center prior to Notification Day.

If you do receive an exclusion notice, do not be devastated by the news. As we noted in the beginning, rejections are inevitable and not everyone fits a program's needs. An exclusion notification simply means that this program is honest and secure enough to follow the rules rather than string you along. Most will probably send out form letters, but if they call, don't get angry or give in to the temptation to say something nasty. Be gracious, and show them that you are a class act. Thank them for the information, express your disappointment, and wish them well. Inform your DCT, and encourage the other placements on your list.

Pressure to make a commitment. The new APPIC rules forbid internships from asking you outright if you rank them first or if you will promise to accept an offer if one is made. Nevertheless, this can happen. If it is your clear first choice, you will probably agree, but if it is number two, then you are in a dilemma.   If they are a strong contender, I would suggest you communicate that fact without implying that you would necessarily accept an offer if it is made. If they really press you, try telling them your program strictly adheres to the APPIC rules, and your DCT will kill you if you reveal your choices. If that doesn't work and they demand a decision, APPIC personnel advise you to agree that they are number one and consult your DCT immediately. This is most likely to happen with a new TD or some other person who does not fully understand the rules. Your DCT should be able to sort it out without you getting hurt.

You may be tempted to assure two or more TDs that they are your "first choice," and promise them both that you will come if invited. DON'T. Doing so is a serious mistake. Besides being dishonest, it can blight your career once you are found out. It is pretty obvious that you were lying when you "first choice" a program, and later turn down their offer.

One TD told me about an applicant who had volunteered that her internship was his first choice, and that he would definitely accept an offer. On Notification Day, he "unexpectedly" received an offer from a place he regarded as more prestigious, and went there instead. He still practices in that area, but, as far as this TD is concerned, he is an unethical person who will never, in his entire life, get any cooperation from her, whether it involves applying for a job, referring patients, asking for subjects, or trying to place students.

You also should be advised that some TDs talk to one another and compare notes about applicants before they make offers. If you have told several training centers in a given area that you rank them first, they may share that information with one another, and none may offer you a position. One year I had a student who applied to several internships in the same city. After interviewing, he rated Southside Hospital first and Northside second, and told Southside they were his first choice. A week later, I got a call from the Training Director at Northside asking me how the student regarded his program. I responded that I thought he ranked it high, but preferred Southside. The Northside TD replied that was what the Southside TD had told him. I realized that we had just passed a credibility test. The student received a bid from Southside, which he promptly accepted.

The commitment letter. If you are clearly sold on a place and if you get sufficient encouragement, you may decide to make a unilateral commitment to accept an offer if it is made. Do not make such an offer without consulting your DCT who can discuss it with the TD and find out if it will help your cause. Some programs disregard such commitments, and others may advise against it (meaning you are not very high on their list). But with some, it may enhance your chances. Shortly after Notification Day, a successful applicant wrote me, "I am now the strongest advocate alive of the commitment letter. I am absolutely convinced that it was the penultimate communication which tipped the scales in my favor..." (Bayon, personal communication, February 11, 1991).

If a program is clearly your first choice, and a firm commitment seems likely to enhance your chances, go for it. In the case of our students, in order to ensure credibility, I personally promise the TD that if the student is offered a fully funded position by noon on Notification Day, he or she will accept it and definitely attend. I also promise the TD that if the student reneges, he or she will be dismembered and his or her body parts sent to the training center at the time the internship was scheduled to begin. So far this has not been necessary.

Uniform Notification Day

Notification Day finally comes on the second Monday in February. It is essential that you have a clear rank ordered list of your preferred placements. Stick with it. Calling is supposed to begin no sooner than 9:00 AM Central Time. This is 10:00 AM in the Eastern Zone, 8:00 AM in the Mountain Zone, 7:00 AM Pacific Time, and 6:00 AM in Hawaii. (I have had students in the East who thought it started at 8:00 AM EST and were suicidal after they received no calls in what they thought were the first two hours.)

Follow these rules:

1. Get everything ready early, such as taking a child to a sitter or day care, getting your list near the phone and so on. Some programs jump the gun and call early.

2. Stay by the phone and keep the line clear. If possible, have a back up phone that you can use to call out.

3. Do not call friends who are also applying. They need to stay by their phones and keep their lines clear. However, it helps to have someone with you who can hold your hand, run errands, deliver messages, and answer the phone while you use the bathroom.

4. If you are going to need to consult with someone else such as a partner or your DCT, make sure the arrangements are in place and you know how to contact this person. Time is of the essence. However, by this time you should have your decisions made, and the need for consultation should be minimal.

5. When you are made an offer you must respond that you will "Accept," "Reject," or "Hold" the offer. If you decide to hold, you have until 4:00 PM CST, to respond. After that time, the offer is automatically rescinded if you have

not accepted. (An internship that will make you an offer only if you agree to accept immediately is violating APPIC guidelines. Tell them so.)

6. Once you Accept an offer, this is a binding commitment. You cannot under any circumstances accept any other offer. Notify all the other programs that you applied to that you are no longer available. If you are holding an offer, notify that program first.

7. You can hold only one offer at a time. If you are holding an offer and a lower ranked program calls, decline. If your first ranked placement calls, accept and release the program whose offer you are holding. Similarly, if a higher ranked program that is not your first choice offers you a position, tell them you will hold it, and immediately release the lower ranked program whose offer you had been holding. (It is all right to hold the two offers for the brief period it takes to notify the lower ranked facility, as long as you do not delay.)

8. If you have not been contacted by your first choice or other high ranking programs after a reasonable time, such as an hour, call them and determine your status. Your call may precipitate an offer because it shows the internship that you are still uncommitted and, obviously, interested. I am convinced that some programs adopt a "wait and see" strategy for at least some of their slots, whereby they identify two or three equally acceptable applicants whose intentions may be uncertain. Instead of calling and committing this slot to one of these candidates, thus risking having it tied up, they may wait and offer it to the first one who calls them.

9. If you committed yourself to a program before Notification Day and you do not hear from them, call them and find out what is going on. I know of at least one case in which the program assumed no call was necessary and left the candidate in suspense all day. Remember, the only

legal offers are those made after 9:00 AM CST on Notification Day.

Whether you accept or decline, do not expect any lengthy conversations with the internship personnel when the initial offers are being made on Notification Day. Time is at a premium and most communications last less than a minute. A typical conversation will go like this:

"Hello, Mr. Tom Cod? This is Dr. Almondine Dover-Sole at Halibut Hospital. I am pleased to offer you a predoctoral psychology internship in our substance abuse track for next Fall."

"I accept."

"Wonderful. You will soon get a letter of confirmation. Goodbye."

After Notification Day

If you have accepted a position, you should write a formal letter of acceptance in which you state your understanding of the agreement that was reached. Moreover, within 72 hours after the close of Notification Day, i.e. by the following Thursday, the Training Director at your internship is supposed to send you and your DCT letters confirming all the details of your appointment. If your understanding agrees with the TD's, you have a "done deal." If not, you and your DCT should get in touch with the TD and discuss the differences. For a contract to be valid, both parties must agree on the terms; the time to discuss any discrepancies is as soon as they are perceived, not when you report to the internship the following September.

For almost everybody, Notification Day signals, at long last, the end of the interminable internship application season. It has consumed months of your life. At last it is over, and you will be surprised how soon it fades from memory. It never fails to amaze me how applicants who were pacing in agitation the week before Notification Day assure their younger colleagues that it was a breeze when they report their experiences at our annual internship panel discussion a week later.

What to do in case of disaster

What should you do if disaster strikes? I hesitate to discuss this subject because it might induce a panic reaction in the more obsessive readers. At the same time, there is information you should have in case of an emergency. If I could, I would have this section published in a separate glass box which you could break open and read in case of emergency. Instead, just skip over this section and read it only if something dreadful happens. If you ask, "What does he mean by dreadful?," it is obvious that it has not happened, so you do not need to read this section. It will just make you anxious. Skip ahead to the section entitled "The bottom line."

Now that we have gotten rid of the voyeurs, I can concentrate on those of you that need help. The first thing to remember is not to panic. Bad things sometimes do happen, but everything somehow gets sorted out, and, more often than not they seem to work out for the best.

One reason why things work out is that after Notification Day, everyone is on the same side. Up to now you may have seen only the competitive side of the TDs; after Notification Day they can resume their normal role as educators trying to give you the best training possible. APPIC, with which you have had minimal contact so far, can be extraordinarily helpful if something goes wrong. If the problem is something you and your DCT can't deal with, APPIC often can and will. Some concrete examples will illustrate.

Failure to obtain a position. For some applicants, disaster means not getting offered an internship on Notification Day. What should you do in this eventuality?

The first thing is to discuss the situation with your DCT or other mentor and diagnose what went wrong. Together you can review your application materials and credentials. Your DCT may be able to call some programs where you applied for feedback. It may be that, professionally or personally, you are simply not ready to go on internship, and this fact was evident to the Selection Committees. If this is the case, painful as it may be, it is probably best that you did not get chosen this year. You need to concentrate on remedying whatever deficits you have so you will be ready at some future date. This may mean additional courses, making further progress on your research, obtaining additional practicum experience, or perhaps getting some personal therapy or counseling.

If you were adequately prepared, perhaps you applied to a poor choice of internships, ones that for some reason were not suitable for a person with your credentials. Perhaps they expect more practicum experience than your program affords. It may be that your credentials did not stand out from the rest, or that you limited your applications to very prestigious institutions with high selection ratios. Perhaps you refused to apply to places that did not meet your exact specifications. Maybe one of your references had doubts about your abilities, or you didn't interview effectively. The point of all this is not to ruminate obsessively about what went wrong, but, with the help of your DCT, mentor and, perhaps, even some of the TDs who rejected your application, to decide whether or not to continue to seek an internship this year. It may be better to spend another year working on your academic goals and building up your credentials.

If you and your advisors decide that this is indeed the best time for you to go on internship, the next task is to match you with one of the remaining unfilled slots that will meet your needs. This is where your DCT and APPIC can help. Every year I get phone calls from good internships that failed to fill all their positions wanting to know if I have any students who have not found a suitable placement. Your DCT may well have received such calls.

However, the most efficient procedure is to access the APPIC Clearinghouse. The Clearinghouse opens the day after Notification Day to facilitate the exchange of information between DCTs and TDs regarding positions that are still available and candidates that are still uncommitted. It continues operating until September 30, because there will always be some candidates who have accepted positions that are unable to attend for various reasons. There are always more slots open than there are qualified applicants to fill them.

The procedures for using the Clearinghouse are spelled out each year in the APPIC Directory. Only DCTs and TDs can access the Clearinghouse, and it must be in writing, by mail or by fax. Information is not accepted over the phone. Training programs report the availability of positions and DCTs report the availability of uncommitted applicants. Your name is not submitted to the Clearinghouse; only the fact that your program has candidates available. The Clearinghouse compiles these reports and distributes them to those APPIC members and subscribers requesting information.

When your DCT gets the report, you survey it for programs that interest you. While some of these internships are ones that are less desirable because of provisional accreditation or location, there are always some first rate placements as well. These come about when applicants hold on to offers and do not release them until it is too late for the internships to recruit people from their alternate list. You or your DCT can contact the programs that interest you directly. Similarly, facilities with openings can call your DCT. Once the initial contact is made, programs and candidates can exchange information and negotiate directly with one another with no further Clearinghouse involvement.

The disappearing internship. If you obtained an internship on Notification Day, and you are nevertheless reading this section reserved for people experiencing disasters, then your emergency may be that you got an internship and it disappeared. Nobody ever told you that this could happen. In fact, this is extremely rare, and we do not mention it because we are afraid that already apprehensive trainees would get absolutely hysterical if they heard about disappearing internships. That is why I did not let the others read this section. But now that it has happened to you, how do we deal with it?

This topic was not covered in the first edition of this book because, until recently, I had never heard of an internship disappearing. This year, I encountered four cases. While this is an infinitesimal proportion of the two thousand plus internships awarded annually... about two tenths of one percent, I figure... it is extremely upsetting to those concerned.

Internships can disappear by acts of God, which are called "natural disasters," and by acts of humans, which logic demands we term "unnatural disasters." In my sample of four cases, unnatural disasters outnumbered the natural kind three to one. We will not draw any theological or philosophical conclusions from this, but simply report on the unnatural kind first.

In 1991, Dr. Kathie Larsen, who was then Chair of APPIC, reported to the membership, "As a number of states are in dire financial straits, training budgets have sometimes been a target of budget cuts. In three cases which came to our attention this summer, internship programs had funding withdrawn or frozen, months after they made offers to interns on calling day" (Larsen,

1991, p. 1). Hiring freezes and layoffs, or, as the British term it "redundancies," are phenomena more common in the 1990s than in recent decades. Ask Mikhail Gorbachev.

Larsen (1991) reported that APPIC intervention was successful in restoring the stipends in two of these cases. The third program was not a member of APPIC, and declined intervention. Moreover, Larsen (1991, p. 1) noted, "The attorneys for this program maintained that acceptance letters specifying dates and the stipend amounts were necessary for the offers made on calling day to be considered binding. The program had not written such letters."

There are several instructive lessons to be drawn from Larsen's comments:

1. Only do business with an APPIC internship;

2. After acceptance, send your internship a letter stipulating your understanding of the conditions of employment, including the dates and stipend;

3. Insist on receiving a formal letter from the internship Training Director specifying the conditions of the appointment, as required by Rule 11 of the APPIC regulations;

4. If you are later told your position is frozen (or if the conditions of employment do not conform to those stipulated in your letter), notify APPIC and ask for their assistance.

If something like this should occur, you will find that the internship's TD and the training faculty will be on your side and will do whatever they can to assist you. They want you as an intern, and they will be utterly appalled and abashed at any abrogation of their good faith agreement by bureaucrats or administrators. They

should welcome the APPIC intervention and anything else that can be done to restore the original
agreement.

Apart from some budgetary problem, could
an internship change its mind after you have
accepted an offer? No. Acceptance is binding on
the training program just as it is on you. Once
you have received the letter, you have an en-
forceable contract. There is only one possible
circumstance that I can imagine whereby an internship might be able to rescind an offer: that
is if someone had submitted a false or fraudulent
application. What would constitute fraud? Misrepresenting one's education or employment history,
forging a transcript or letter of recommendation,
concealing a felony conviction if asked... these
are the sorts of things that could conceivably lead
an internship to reconsider and prevail in the
event of a lawsuit (Hollander, 1990). If a candidate has honestly supplied all the information
required, then the internship's acceptance letter
makes it a "done deal."

But what about natural disasters? Well,
these do occur; in fact, while this chapter was
being written, there were three major earthquakes
in Southern California. However, even catastro-
phes somehow seem to work out for the best. One
year, one of my students seemed to have nothing
but bad luck. A thoroughly congenial chap, "Hard
luck Sam" had excellent credentials and superb
letters. He should have had no difficulties, but
unfortunately his first choice was one which receives well over 100 applications. Admission there
always requires good luck, and Sam's seemed in
short supply. The TD was most supportive and
told Sam that he had been one of the first alternates; there were simply not enough slots available to make him an offer.

Sam was disappointed but he accepted a
position at his second choice and made the best of
it. Some months later Sam called me in a panic. As
he and his family were packing to move, he had

received a call from his internship; there had been a natural disaster and much of the institution had been badly damaged. The patients were being transferred elsewhere, and the facility would be closed for at least a year for repairs.

I called the TD at Sam's first choice and told her about his latest hard luck. I reminded her of all the positive things she had said about Sam, and suggested that it might be possible for her to arrange to have Sam transferred to her program along with his stipend. It took some doing, but eventually it was all worked out. Thanks to the natural disaster, Sam ended up at his first choice where he had a superb year.

The bottom line

If you are not experiencing any post-Notification Day trauma and skipped the previous section, you can resume reading now.

Applying for internships is difficult but not impossible. It is stressful, but there is no reason why you should not be able to cope with it successfully now that you understand what it is all about. The important thing to remember is that everybody concerned is seeking the optimal match between interns and programs in order to achieve the best possible educational experience for all concerned.

Many applicants experience needless anxiety because of unrealistic expectancies. Put aside any irrational concerns, and you will be able to cope with the real issues effectively.

No matter what sort of internship you decide is best for you, you want to make the best possible impression. First, make sure you are ready for internship. Develop your skills and credentials to the utmost. Take the right courses, work hard and get good grades. Read on your own and develop your knowledge of all things clinical. Do well in a variety of practicum settings; be the person who is responsive to supervision, who can be relied on to keep cool in a crisis, and who cheerfully handles their share of the tough tasks. Produce quality research and get it published. Have a dissertation project approved and in progress. In short, do everything you can to be the kind of student you will want to supervise in the years to come.

Once you have established your qualifications, review your priorities and preferences, investigate the various internships and select those that best meet your needs. Then go for it. Make the best possible presentation via your CV, letters and interviews. In your interviews, obtain the data you need to make your decision and be honest and forthright with the internship training faculties. Work with your DCT, discuss your options with the internship TDs, and convince the programs that you have what it takes to succeed. I hope you get what you are looking for and that this book has helped.

REFERENCES

American Psychological Association. (1986). Accreditation handbook. Washington, DC: Author.

American Psychological Association. (1989). Directory of the American Psychological Association, 1989 Edition. (Vols. 1-2). Washington, DC: Author.

American Psychological Association Committee on Accreditation. (1991). APA accredited predoctoral internships for doctoral training in psychology: 1991. American Psychologist, 46, 1308-1331.

Association of Psychology Postdoctoral and Internship Centers. (1991a). Directory: Internship and postdoctoral programs in professional psychology 20th ed. Washington, D.C.: Author.

Association of Psychology Postdoctoral and Internship Centers. (1991b). Preliminary pre-doctoral summaries. APPIC Newsletter, 16(2), 47.

Belar, C.D., Bieliauskas, L.A., Larsen, K.G., Mensh, I. N., Poey, K., & Roehlke, A.J.. (Eds.). (1987). Proceedings of the National Conference on Internship Training in Psychology. Washington, DC: Association of Psychology Internship Centers.

Belar, C., & Orgel, S. (1980). Survival guide for intern applicants. Professional Psychology, 11, 672-675.

Blom, B. E. (1990). Remarks from the editor. APIC Newsletter, 15(2), 5-7.

Blom, B. E. (1991). Remarks from the editor. APPIC Newsletter, 16(2), 2–3.

Blom, B. E., Pederson, S. L., & Klepac, R. K. (1990). The computerized internship matching pilot study. Further results, cautions and excuses. APIC Newsletter, 15(1), 20–22.

Burt, C. E. (1985). Reflections on interviewing for internship. Clinical Psychologist, 38, 91–93.

Dana, R. H., & May, W. T. (Eds.). (1987). Internship training in professional psychology. Washington, DC: Hemisphere.

Douce, L. A. (1990). Intern selection advisory. APIC Newsletter, 15(1), 59–60.

Eggert, M. A., Laughlin, P. R., Hutzell, R. R., Stedmen, J. M., Solway, K. S., & Carrington, C. H. (1987). The psychology internship marketplace today. Professional Psychology: Research and Practice, 18, 165–171.

Fox, R. E. (1990). The history of the APIC selection process: A personal prequel. APIC Newsletter, 15(1), 27–28.

Fox, R. E. (1991). Improvements still needed in selection process. APIC Newsletter, 16(2), 33–36.

Gavzer, B. (1992, June 14). Fly smart. Parade Magazine, pp. 4–6.

Grace, W. C. (1985). Evaluating a prospective clinical internship: Tips for the applicant. Professional Psychology: Research and Practice, 15, 475–480.

Hersh, J. B., & Poey, K. (1984). A proposed interviewing guide for intern applicants. Professional Psychology: Research and Practice, 15, 3-5.

Hollander, P. A. (1990). Internships and the law: Questions and answers. APIC Newsletter, 15 (1), 56-57.

Jacob, M. C. (1987). Managing the internship application: Advice from an exhausted but content survivor. The Counseling Psychologist, 15, 146-155.

Kingsley, K. (1985). Reflections on internship year. Clinical Psychologist, 38,, 93-94.

Larsen, K. G. (1991). Chair's column. APPIC Newsletter, 16(2), 1-2.

Larsen, K. G., & Klepac, R. K. (1991). How to survive intern calling day: A guide for training directors. APPIC Newsletter, 16(2), 32-33.

May, T. M., & Dana, R. H. (1990). Issues concerning the internship selection process. APIC Newsletter, 15(1), 29-32.

May, T. M., Rice, K., & Birckhead, L. (1990). A current perspective on intern selection: The state of the art. APIC Newsletter, 15(2), 37-42.

Miller, R. K., & Van Rybroek, G.J. (1988). Internship letters of recommendation: Where are the other 90%? Professional Psychology: Research and Practice, 19, 115-117.

Monti, P. M. (1985). Interviewing for internships. The Behavior Therapist, 10, 205-206.

Ochroch, R. (1990).   The need for half-time
    internships: Affirmative action on behalf of
    parents of young children. APIC Newslet-
    ter, 15(2), 35–37.

Stanford University Career Planning and Placement
    Center (1988). How to write your resume.
    Stanford, CA: Author.

Stedman, J. M. (1989). The history of the APIC
    selection process. APIC Newsletter, 14 (2),
    35–43.

Stedman, J. M., Costello, R. M., Gaines, Jr.,
    T., Solway, K., Zimet, C., & Carrington,
    C. (1990). Intern supply and demand: The
    rest of the story. APIC Newsletter, 15(1),
    33–43.

Sundberg, N. D., Taplin, J. R., & Tyler, L. E.
    (1983). Introduction to clinical psychology.
    Englewood Cliffs, NJ: Prentice Hall.

Weiner, E. (1990, January 21). Why plane travel
    isn't always fast. New York Sunday Times,
    National News, pp. 1, 15.

Winiarski, M. (1986). Applying for internship.
    Unpublished manuscript, Psychology Depart-
    ment, Florida State University, Tallahassee.

Zimet, C. N. (1990). Chair's column. APIC
    Newsletter, 15(2), 4-5

Zimet, C. N. (1991). Chair's column. APPIC
    Newsletter, 16(1), 1-3.

APPIC POLICY: INTERNSHIP OFFERS AND ACCEPTANCES (REVISED 1991)

1. **These policies must be made known to all students applying to APPIC member internship programs, and to all others affected by these policies.**

    a. APPIC member programs must include a copy of these policies in internship materials sent to applicants.

    b. Directors of APPIC internship programs must insure that all people involved in recruiting or selecting interns are familiar with the policies, the need to communicate policies to applicants, and the importance of adhering to the policies.

    c. Directors of academic training programs (universities and professional schools) whose students intend to apply to APPIC member internship programs are requested to insure that these policies are understood and adhered to by their students.

2. **Internship program directors must inform applicants who are excluded from consideration as early as possible in the process, and no later than one week before selection day.**

    a. Students who remain under consideration may be notified that they remain under consideration after others have been excluded.

    b. No other information (such as agency's ranking of the applicant; status as alternate/first choice, etc.) may be communicated to applicants prior to selection day.

3. **No internship offers in any form may be extended by agencies before the beginning of selection day.**

    a. The only information that agencies may communicate to applicants prior to this time is whether or not the applicant remains under consideration for admission (see item 2). The spirit of this item precludes any communication of an applicant's status prior to the time above, however "veiled" or indirect such communication might be.

    b.   "Alternates" may be fully informed of their status any time after the start of selection day. Applicants may not be told whether they are considered alternates or first choices prior to that time.

    c.   Internship programs may not solicit information regarding an applicant's ranking of programs or his/her intention to accept or decline an offer of admission until after that offer is officially tendered.

4.   **Applicants must reply to all offers no later than the closing time on selection day**

    a.   This deadline applies to all offers including those to applicants who are initially considered "alternates" and are subsequently extended an offer any time prior to end of selection day.

    b.   Agencies may inquire as to the applicant's progress towards making a decision at any time after an offer is formally extended. Under no circumstances, however, may an agency implicitly or explicitly threaten to rescind an offer if a decision is not made prior to the end of selection day (except as noted in item 6.)

    c.   It is in everyone's best interest that applicants make and communicate decisions to accept or reject each offer as quickly as possible.

    d.   Any offer that has not been accepted is void as of the ending hour of selection day.

5.   **An applicant must respond immediately to each offer tendered in one of three ways. The offer may be accepted, rejected, or "held."**

    a.   Accepting the offer constitutes a binding agreement between applicant and internship program;

    b.   Refusing the offer terminates all obligations on either side and frees the internship program to offer the position to another applicant;

    c.   Holding the offer means that the offer remains valid until the applicant notifies the program of rejection or acceptance, or until the end of selection day.

6. **Applicants may "Hold" no more than one active offer at a time.**

    a.   If an applicant is holding an offer from one program and receives an offer from a more-preferred program, s/he may accept or "hold" the second offer provided that the less-preferred program is notified immediately that the applicant is rejecting the previously-held offer.

    b.   If a program confirms that an applicant is holding more than one offer, the program is free to withdraw their previously-tendered offer of acceptance, and to offer that position to another applicant after the offending applicant is notified of that decision.

7. **An offer of acceptance to an applicant is valid only if the applicant has not already accepted an offer of admission to another program.**

    a.   An applicant's verbal acceptance of an offer constitutes a binding agreement between the applicant and the program that may not be reversed unilaterally by either party.

    b.   Before programs extend an offer, they must first explicitly inquire whether the applicant has already accepted an offer elsewhere. If so, no offer may be tendered.

    c.   A program may in no way suggest that an applicant renege on previously-accepted offers.

    d.   If an applicant who has accepted an offer receives a second offer, s/he is obligated to refuse the second offer and inform the agency that s/he is already committed elsewhere.

    e.   Any offer accepted subsequent to a prior commitment is automatically null and void, even if the offering agency is unaware of the prior acceptance and commitment.

8. **When applicant accepts an offer of admission, s/he is urged to immediately inform all other internship programs at which s/he is still under consideration that s/he is no longer available.**

9. **Applicants who have not accepted a position prior to the end of selection day may receive offers of admission after that deadline.**

    a.   Applicants should be prepared to accept or reject such late offers quickly, since most other deliberations should have already taken place

    b.   Programs may legitimately place short but reasonable deadlines for responses to such late offers.

10. **Once a program has filled all available positions, all candidates remaining in their applicant pool must be notified that they are no longer under consideration.**

    a.   Applicants who have not notified the agency that they have accepted a position elsewhere and who have not been selected by the agency should be notified by phone as soon as all positions are filled.

    b.   If an applicant cannot be reached by phone, s/he should be so notified by letter postmarked no later than 72 hours after the end of selection day.

11. **Internship training directors should document their verbal agreement with each applicant in a letter postmarked no later than 72 hours following the end of selection day.**

    a.   The letter should be addressed to the applicant, and should include confirmation of conditions of the appointment, such as stipend, fringe benefits, and the date on which the internship begins.

    b.   A copy of that letter should be sent simultaneously to the applicant's academic program director.

12. **Applicants who receive offers which do not comply with these policies or who in other ways detect violations of these policies by an APPIC member program are urged to request compliance with APPIC policies from the program representative.**

    a.   Applicants should immediately report any problems unresolved after such request to his/her academic program director.

    b.   Academic program directors are urged to contact internship training directors immediately regarding such unresolved problems.

c. Such compliance problems should be resolved through consultation among applicant, internship program, and academic training director whenever possible.

d. Problems not amenable to resolution through such consultation should be reported as soon as possible to the APPIC Standards and Review Committee at the address listed at the end of this document.

13. **Internship directors who become aware of violations of policies on the part of students, academic training directors, or other internship directors are urged to immediately request compliance to the policies.**

a. Internship directors are urged to contact academic training program directors immediately regarding problems that remain unresolved after such a request for compliance.

b. Internship program directors who become aware of violations of these policies by other internship programs should urge the applicant and academic training directors involved to follow the procedures outlined in 12 a-d above, and/or to directly contact the other internship director.

c. Such compliance problems should be resolved through consultation among applicant, internship programs, and academic training director whenever possible.

d. Failure to resolve compliance problems through consultation should be reported to the APPIC Standards and Review Committee.

14. **All reported violations of these policies will be considered by the APPIC Standards and Review Committee (ASRC). ASRC policies are described in the _APPIC Director_. Violations of these policies should be reported to:**

Chair, APPIC Standards and Review Committee
733 15th Street, N.W., Suite 717
Washington, DC 20005
(202) 347-0022   FAX (202) 393-0079

APPENDIX TWO

INTERNSHIP PROGRAMS RECEIVING 100 OR MORE COMPLETED APPLICATIONS IN 1990/91

CALIFORNIA

La Jolla: Univ. of Calif., San Diego (125/5)

Los Angeles: Kaiser-Permanente Medical Care Program (103/4); LAC - USC Medical Center (108/4); Univ.of Calif., LA (116/6).

Orange: Univ. of Calif., Irvine Medical Center (100/3).

Palo Alto: VA Medical Center, (162/14).

San Francisco: VA Medical Center, (105/3).

COLORADO

Denver: Univ. of Colorado Health Sciences Center (110/8).

CONNECTICUT

New Haven: Yale University School of Medicine (108/23).

DISTRICT OF COLUMBIA

Washington D.C.: Commission on Mental Health Services (125/12).

GEORGIA

Augusta: VA Medical Center/Medical College of Georgia Consortium (140/9).

ILLINOIS

Chicago: Children's Memorial Hospital (100/3); Cook County Hospital (130/5); Illinois Masonic Medical Center (130/4); Northwestern University Medical Center (100/9); Rush-Presbyterian-St. Luke's Medical Center (175/8).

INDIANA

Indianapolis: IU School of Medicine (105/9).

MARYLAND

Baltimore: Homewood Hospital (130/4).

Note. The first number in parentheses is the number of completed applications received; the second is the number of full time fully funded internships available. Data from APPIC (1991a).

MASSACHUSETTS

Belmont: McLean Hospital (Adult)/Harvard Medical School (150/10).

Boston: Beth Israel Hospital (100/5); Harvard Medical School/Mass. Mental Health Center (135/9); Judge Baker/Childrens Hospital (116/13); Tufts Univ. School of Medicine/Boston VA Consortium (113/11).

Cambridge: Cambridge Hospital/Harvard Medical School (170/9).

NEW YORK

Albany: Albany Psychology Internship Consortium (100/7).

Bronx: Albert Einstein College of Medicine (142/10).

Glen Oaks: Long Island Jewish Medical Center (128/12).

New York: Beth Israel Medical Center (175/5); Columbia Presbyterian Medical Center (200/7); New York Univ., Bellevue Hospital Center (300/16); Postgraduate Center for Mental Health (120/7); The St. Lukes/Roosevelt Hospital Center (155/15).

NORTH CAROLINA

Chapel Hill: UNC School of Medicine (170/10)

Durham: Duke Univ. Medical Center (150/8).

SOUTH CAROLINA

Charleston: Medical Univ.of SC (150/14).

TEXAS

Houston: Univ. of Texas Medical School, Houston (105/9).

TENNESSEE

Memphis: Univ. of Tennessee, Memphis (100/9)

Nashville: Vanderbilt University/VA Medical Center (110/0).

WASHINGTON

Seattle: Seattle VA Medical Center (102/5); University of Washington (195/13).

APPENDIX THREE

A SAMPLE CURRICULUM VITAE

Curriculum Vitae

Rosa Thorne
(Formerly Rosa Cholla)

Addresses

Home: 2702 Elm Street
University City,
West Idabama 82046
(111) 222-3333
(Leave message)

Work: Psychology Clinic
ML 102, West Idabama
State University
University City, WI 82032
(111) 888-777, Ext 240

Personal Data

Birthplace: Santo Loco, Costa Rojo
Citizenship: U.S. (naturalized 10/1/88)
Birthdate: 2/27/65
Marital Status: Married
Ethnicity: Hispanic
Social Security: 222-33-4444

Education

1989
to
Present

Doctoral Candidate, Psychology Department
West Idabama State University

Major: Clinical Psychology
Minor: Nutrition
Dissertation Topic: The influence of grain
    price fluctuations on post-tramautic stress
    disorders among Midwestern farmers.
    (Prospectus Defended: July 4, 1990)
Major Professor: B. J. Mentor, Ph.D.
Comprehensive Examination: Passed,
    December 25,1989
Areas of Concentration: Psychopathology,
    Food psychology

218

1986
to
1989
	Master of Science, Psychology Department
	West Idabama State University
	   Major: Clinical Psychology
	   Major Professor: Mary Grayhead, Ph.D.
	   Thesis Title: Personality changes
	      resulting from pesticide exposure in
	      rural children.

1981
to
1985
	Bachelor of Science, _magna_ _cum_ _laude_
	Horatio Alger College
	Collegetown, West Idabama
	   Major: Psychology
	   Minor: Home Economics
	   Honors: Phi Beta Kappa, Sigma Xi

Other Educational Experience

February 12, 1989: Advanced 8 PF Test workshop (6 hrs.)
          Presented by Raymond Stenscore, Ph.D.
          Sponsored by American Personality Association,
          Central City, West Idabama

April 18, 1988: Eating Disorders Workshop (8 hrs.)
          Presented by Duncan Donut, Ph.D.
          Sponsored by West Idabama Psychology Association,
          University City, WI

Special Skills

Native fluency in Spanish.

Professional Affiliations

West Idabama Psychology Association
        Student Member
        Vice President, 1988

American Association of Food Psychologists
        Associate Member

Professional Credentials

Licensed Food Psychologist, West Idabama (License #000248)

OBTAINING A PSYCHOLOGY INTERNSHIP

Supervised Clinical Experience

June, 1990
to
Present

Psychology Trainee
University City Community Mental Health Center
University City, West Idabama

Duties: Outpatient based assessment and therapy with adult, adolescent and child populations. Client population includes a variety of developmental, anxiety, mood, personality and organic disorders. Complete assessments performed for learning disabilities, neuropsychological, attention deficit hyperactivity and personality disorders. Therapy experience includes group, family, conjoint, and individual using an eclectic approach. (20 hrs/wk - estimate 1000 hrs. by August, 1991)

Supervisor: Alice Sage, Ph.D., ABPP

June, 1988
to
May, 1990

Psychology Trainee
West Idabama State Hospital
Central City, West Idabama

Duties: Inpatient based assessment and therapy with an adult population. Responsibilities include screening admissions using objective and projective devices; intellectual and personality testing as requested by resident psychiatrists; and leading assertiveness training groups. (10 hrs/wk, 1000 hrs. total)

Supervisors: George Thyme, Ph.D. and Mary Marjoram, Ph.D.

June, 1989
to
Present

Crisis Management Unit Team Member
West Idabama State University
University City, West Idabama

Duties: On site intervention and evaluation of psychotic, suicidal and homicidal crises; assess dangerousness and need for hospitalization; transport clients to psychiatric receiving facilities with a member of the West Idabama State University Police Department. (On call for 24 hours, roughly 6 days a month.)

Supervisor: Delilah Sampson, Ph.D.

June, 1987	Psychology Trainee
to	West Idabama State University
May, 1988	Campus Psychology Clinic

Duties: Individual, family and marital therapy involving clients with wide variety of presenting problems (including: child management, marital issues, social skill deficits, low self-esteem, substance abuse, depression, stress management, impulse and anger control, and learning disabilities. Assessments for learning disabilities, attention deficit hyperactivity disorder, behavior problems and emotional problems. (10 hrs/wk for 80 weeks = 800 hrs)

Supervisor: Sara Nutmeg, Ph.D.

Total hours of supervised clinical experience = 2800

Instrument Competence

Type of Test	Number Administered and Interpreted
Intellectual Abilities	
WISC-R	75
WAIS-R	120
Stanford Binet (4th Ed)	20
Woodcock-Johnson Tests of Cognitive Ability	25
Achievement Tests	
Wide-Range Achievement Test	50
Woodcock-Johnson Test of Achievement Revised	25
Personality	
Rorschach (Exner Systems)	30
Thematic Apperception Test	20
California Psychological Inventory	25
MMPI	75
Neuropsychological	
Luria Nebraska Neuropsychological Test Battery	20

(In addition I have been exposed to and administered five or less Columbia Mental Maturity Examinations, Rosensweig Picture Frustration Studies and Cattell 16-PF Inventories.)

Teaching Experience

June, 1989   General Psychology for Honors Students
   to   Freshman/Sophomore Level Course
Present   Department of Psychology
                West Idabama State University

Duties: Responsible for all phases of teaching including the preparation and administration of lectures, selection of reading materials and
assignments, construction of examinations, and the assignment of course
grades.

May, 1988   Sensation and Perception
   to   Junior/Senior Level Course
August, 1988   Department of Psychology
                West Idabama State University

Duties: Responsible for all phases of teaching including the preparation and administration of lectures, the selection of reading materials
and assignments, the development of experiments to demonstrate sensory
and perceptual principles, the construction of examinations, and the
assignment of course grades.

August, 1987   General Psychology
   to   Freshman/Sophomore Level Course
May, 1988   Department of Psychology
                West Idabama State University

Duties: Responsible for all phases of teaching including the preparation and administration of lectures, the selection of reading materials
and assignments, the construction of examinations, and the assignment of
course grades.

Research

June, 1989   Dissertation in progress.
to
Present   This study is using a time series analysis to investigate the association of fluctuations in grain prices on the incidence of post-traumatic stress disorders among Midwestern farmers, covarying for interest rates, in comparison with the incidence of PTSD among service workers in the same area.

My prospectus was defended July 4, 1990 and data collection is almost complete. I anticipate defending the dissertation before leaving for internship.

June, 1987   Research Assistant
to   B. J. Mentor, Ph.D.
May, 1989
Worked 10 hrs/wk on Dr. Mentor's NAA-funded Epidemiological study of nutrition and stress in rural Americans. In the course of this research I administered 350 Structured Clinical Interviews and was responsible for coding Demographic Data.

June, 1988   Master's Thesis Research
to
May, 1989   In this study I compared the Eight-Personality Factor (8PF) profiles of 25 male and 25 female adolescent farm children who had been exposed to significant levels of malathion and DDT as children with matched samples of suburban children from the same school. As predicted by Bovine's Dissipation theory, the exposed male children were higher on scales assessing Threshia and Harvestia and the suburban boys were lower in Reaping. No differences were noted for the girls.

Publications and Presentations

Thorne, R.C. & Grayhead, M. (1989). Effects of herbicide exposure on personality factors in rural adolescents: A test of Bovine's hypotheses. Journal of Food Psychology, 12, 432-441.

Thorne, R.C. (1989, May). Environmental influences on personality development. Paper presented at the meeting of the West Idabama Psychological Association, Central City, West Idabama.

Under Submission
Mentor, B. J., Grayhead, M., & Thorne, R.C. Nutritional stresses in adolescence. Chapter to appear in C. Bovine and B. Allspice (Eds.), Comprehensive handbook of food psychology to be published by the West Idabama State University Press.

References
B. J. Mentor, Ph.D.
Professor of Psychology
Psychology Department
West Idabama State University
University City, West Idabama 82032

Alice Sage, Ph.D.
Chief Psychologist
University City Community Mental Health Center
2102 River Road
University City, West Idabama 82066

Sigmund Spinach, Ph.D.
Director of Clinical Training
Psychology Department
West Idabama State University
University City, West Idabama 82032

APPENDIX FOUR

A SAMPLE TRAVEL PLANNER

TRAVEL PLANNER

Traveler(s)_____

Destination:_____

Purpose:_____

Duration:_____

===

Day #   Day: Dates:

Plan:

===

Air:

            Place   Time   Carrier   Flt No.

Leave_____

Arrive_____

Leave_____

Arrive_____

Leave_____

Arrive_____

Ground:

Carrier:_____   Confirm #_____

Hotel:_____   Confirm #_____

Address:_____   Phone No:_____

Rate:_____   How Paid:_____

Contacts:

1)Name:_____Phone No._____

Where:_____   When:_____

2)Name:_____Phone No._____

Where:_____   When:_____

OBTAINING A PSYCHOLOGY INTERNSHIP

==
Day #   Day: Dates:
Plan:
==
Schedule:

_____

_____

_____

_____

_____

_____

Contacts:

1)Name:_____Phone No._____
Where:_____   When:_____

2)Name:_____Phone No._____
Where:_____   When:_____

3)Name:_____Phone No._____
Where:_____   When:_____

Air:
              Place   Time   Carrier   Flt No.

Leave_____
Arrive_____

Leave_____
Arrive_____

Leave_____
Arrive_____

APPENDIX FIVE

QUESTIONS INTERVIEWERS ASK
INTERN APPLICANTS

These last two appendices are placed at the end so you can find them easily. If you have a few minutes while you are waiting for an interview, you may want to review these questions.

Hersh and Poey (1985) provide an outline of questions that may asked by internship directors. Their list of topics to be covered is rather formal, and represents a systematic exploration of your experience in various areas such as individual adult therapy, group therapy, inpatient, outpatient, assessment, supervision, and so on. In each area, you are asked about your past experience, orientation, work style and areas that need improvement. Some TDs use this outline so you should familiarize yourself with it and be prepared to respond to the questions posed.

The interviews my students have experienced have often been less structured and more personal. In standard employment interviews, personal topics are off limits, but many TDs do not feel that this prohibition extends to internship applicants and will inquire about personal matters. The big question, which is off limits but may be asked covertly, is, "Are you really interested in this internship? If we make you an offer, will you accept?"

Remember that most interviewers are as interested in <u>how</u> you respond as they are in the actual content of your answers. Humor, flexibility, good eye contact, and a firm handshake are important.

Personal/Professional Questions

--How did you become interested in psychology?

--How did you become interested in (specific professional/research interest areas)?

--What would you be doing if you were not in psychology?

--What do you see as your personal strengths and weaknesses? How do they influence your work? What have you done to deal with your shortcomings?

--Have you ever been in therapy? How did this affect how you conducted therapy?

--What are your goals after internship? In five years?

Purely Personal Questions

--Tell me about yourself.

--What do you see as your personal strengths and weaknesses? Who are you, personally?

--Tell me about your family. Are you married? Do you have any children? Tell me about them. What arrangements will you be making for them while you are interning?

--Tell me about your family problems.

--What was the worst thing about your father? Your mother?

--What do you do in your spare time?

--How is your health?

Questions About Your Credentials

--What were your GRE scores? GPA?

--How many graduate programs accepted you?

--Why did you choose your training program?

--Why should we accept you over the other equally qualified candidates?

--What do you have to contribute to us?

Questions About Research

--What is your dissertation topic? How is your research progressing? Where do you see it going?

--How did you get interested in that topic?

--What is the clinical relevance of your research?

Questions About Assessment

--Tell us about an instrument with which you feel competent.

--What is your opinion of projective techniques?

--What Rorschach scoring system do you use? Why?

--What do you think of this Rorschach response?

--What is you opinion of MMPI-2?

--Comment on this MMPI profile.

--What further assessment training or experiences do you need?

Questions About Treatment

--What is your greatest strength as a therapist?

--What type of client is most difficult for you to work with? What type of feelings do you have toward such cases? How do these feelings interfere with your treatment?

--What is your orientation in therapy? What do you think of [dynamic, behavioral, etc.] approaches?

--What experience have you had with [family, group, inpatient, etc.] treatment?

--Talk about a therapy case you had. How did you conceptualize the case? What was most effective?

--What sorts of supervisors have you had? What type of supervision is best for you?

--What further therapy training or experiences do you need?

Questions About Clients

--What sorts of clients have you worked with? Which were you most comfortable with? Effective? Least comfortable? Least effective?

--Have you worked with clients such as we have here?

--What is your opinion of the most recent diagnostic nomenclature? How could it be improved?

Questions About Ethics

--Tell me about an ethical problem you have been faced with and how you handled it.

--Describes situation and asks ethical implications

Questions Dealing With Recruiting

--What can we do to make you want to come here?

--How do you see us as fitting with your goals?

--Which of your interest areas are (are not) addressed by our program?

--Where else have you applied and what attracted you to these places?

--Why would someone from an ("X-oriented") department want to come to a ("Y-oriented") program?

--What attracts you most to our internship?

Others

--What else would you like me to know that is not apparent from your CV?

--What is the one question you would like me to ask you?

--What do you hope we will not find out about you?

--I notice you did not take any coffee. Have you been reading Megargee's book? Are you the kind of person who always "does things by the book"? (New question that followed publication of the first edition in 1990.)

APPENDIX SIX

QUESTIONS INTERN APPLICANTS
CAN ASK INTERVIEWERS

Questions Regarding The Setting/Professional

--What are you looking for in an intern?

--What does an intern do during a typical work week?

✶--Do you anticipate any staff or program changes for the next year?

--What is the relation between psychology and other disciplines?

--Are interns here regarded as employees or students?

--What is the balance between service and training? Does funding for the program depend on fees generated by the interns and staff?

✶--How does the program here compare with where you interned?

--Does this program encourage specialization or diversification in training?

--What are the possibilities of doing research during the internship? Would you say there is a research focus here?

-(To a present intern): What do you like most about this internship? What do you like least?

--Is this a congenial setting? How do trainees and staff get along?

Questions Regarding The Setting/Personal

--What is the cost of living here? Does the program provide health care?

--Are any changes in stipends or benefits expected?

--Is day care for children difficult to find? How are the schools in this area?

--How available are jobs in my spouse's field?

--What is the availability of affordable housing here?

--Do many interns take outside jobs during the intern year?

Questions Regarding Rotations

--Do you anticipate any changes in the rotations being offered next year?

--How are rotations determined? Are they fixed or flexible?

--Do interns negotiate for rotations?

--What are the common presenting problems on the [insert] rotation? What is the typical duration of treatment? What is the ratio of therapy to assessment?

--(To an intern): What rotations do you regard as being truly outstanding? Which ones should you avoid?

Questions Regarding Assessment

--Is there a standard assessment battery? Are projectives used much?

--What are the opportunities for neuropsych assessment?

Questions Regarding Therapy

--What opportunities are there for [family, group etc.] therapy?

--Are there opportunities to conduct groups on the inpatient unit? What kinds of groups are done? Supportive, problem-centered, insight-oriented?

--How many long-term clients does an intern carry?

--Are interns expected or encouraged to have personal therapy? If so, who provides it and what are the goals?

Questions Regarding Supervision

--How many supervisors does an intern have? How are they assigned?

--Is all supervision provided on site? Is supervision on an individual or group basis?

--How much and what type (audio, video, live) supervision is provided?

--What are the theoretical orientations of the supervisors? Which is predominant?

Questions Regarding Didactics

--What types of seminars are offered? What are some typical topics?

Questions Regarding Future Opportunities

--Where do your interns go after finishing their internship? Where are some of your former interns now? What kinds of job opportunities are there for psychologists in this area?

--Does the internship play an active role in trying to place its graduates?

EDWIN I. MEGARGEE

Edwin I. Megargee received his BA magna cum laude from Amherst College in 1958 and his Ph.D. in clinical psychology from the University of California at Berkeley in 1964. The recipient of national awards for outstanding research in the areas of correctional psychology and assessment. He has been an officer of a number of professional organizations.

As Director of Clinical Training at Florida State University, Megargee has personally visited dozens of internships throughout the United States and has presented workshops and classes on how to apply for internship.